Design by Dawn Lewandowski

Printed in the United States of America

ISBN 978-1-60643-974-6

THE HIDDEN MILLIONAIRE

Table of Contents

Acknowledgements

Introduction 1
    Birth of a Philosophy
    "Entrepreneur"—What It Means to Me
    Yes! There Really Is a Formula for Success
    You Have Heard It All Before but...

Chapter One: The Entrepreneurial Mindset 7
    Find Your Passion
    The Entrepreneurial Equation: Personality Times
Five Equals...

Chapter Two: Business as Pleasure 13
    A Charmed Life
    The Young Entrepreneur
    Batter Up!
    New Ideas Are All Around You

Chapter Three: Being Aggressive Pays 25
    The Autograph Diaries
    Be Friendly, Polite and Aggressive
    The Accidental Business

Table of Contents continued

Chapter Four: Striving for Knowledge 33
       The Face That Launched a Thousand...Chats!
       Other People's Money
       A Sudden Change in Plans
       The Good Doctor

Chapter Five: The Fearlessness of Success 45
       The WorldCom Disaster
       Stepping Up to the Plate
       The Cool Blue Solution
       Don't Reinvent the Wheel—Make It Better

Chapter Six: Starting Small, Thinking Big 55
       Turning the Tables
       Giving "Good Phone"—An Essential Tool for
Success
       Virtual World versus Real World
       The Middleman Factor
       Failure Is NOT an Option
       Measure by Deeds, not Dollars

Chapter Seven: Achieving Balance 65
       A Friend for Life
       The Importance of Balance
       Balance and the Beast
       Making Things Work
       The Power of Perseverance

Table of Contents continued

Chapter Eight: Business Outside the Internet Box . . 77
   The Emancipation of Justin
   An Interesting Idea
   Thinking Outside the Box
   Affiliate Income, Inc.
   Hidden Millionaires Revealed

Chapter Nine: Trusting My Instincts 99
   Lights, Camera, Action!
   Take Two
   My First Seminar
   The Teacher Is Inspired
   Learning While Working
   Go With Your Gut

Chapter Ten: Investing in Yourself 115
   Direct Response Partnerships
   Back to the Studio
   You Are Your Best Investment

Chapter Eleven: Building a Reliable Network 123
   No Man (or Woman) Is an Island
   The Incomparable LaTesha Burroughs
   A "Gearhead" and a Good Friend
   The Dream Team
   There's No Substitute for Family
   Surround Yourself With Good People

Table of Contents continued

Chapter Twelve: With Success Comes Responsibility ..
. 131
     Pay It Forward
     Bustin' Out the Santa Suit
     Christmas for Kids
     Children Are the Future
     A Life Less Ordinary

Conclusion: Going Forward 145
     Develop an Entrepreneurial Mindset
     New Ideas Are All Around You
     Be Aggressive
     Strive to Acquire Knowledge
     Don't Be Afraid to Take Risks
     Start Small but Think Big
     Balance Work and Life
     Never Allow Yourself to Become Complacent
     Trust Your Instincts
     Invest in Yourself
     With Success Comes Responsibility
     Build a Reliable Network

Epilogue 165

Index

Acknowledgements

I would like to dedicate this book to my father, Roger Morrison, the best father anyone could ask for. He has always provided our family with everything we needed, and more both financially and emotionally. He showed me how good character and wise decision-making are among the most important things in life. I truly believe I inherited his entrepreneurial spirit, and for that, I am forever grateful. My dad is a great man who taught by example that giving is always better than receiving. Without him, I would be nowhere and certainly not a successful entrepreneur.

I would also like to dedicate this to my mother, Sheila Morrison. From the moment I was born, my mom has been by my side, supporting everything I do and guiding me in the right direction. She willingly gave up her career to stay home with her children. For this, I respect her highly, and I am so thankful to have her with me every day of my life. She has taught me so much, and helped me through so many things. She was a pivotal force in helping me write this book and her contribution is priceless. I love her with all of my heart.

I would also like to thank my brother, Adrian Morrison, the best brother in the world. He remains a positive inspiration for me in all aspects of my life and he is the one person who always motivates me and believes in everything I do. Adrian has listened and learned from me over the years and now runs his own successful

Acknowledgements

business. He was a huge proponent of me writing this book and sharing my story with the world.

I also must mention my sister, Brittain, who works with me daily running my various businesses. She enjoys learning and taking care of the things I am unable to take care of and is simply a great person who is a wonderful business associate and colleague as well as a loving supportive sister. I love her very much, and I know I can depend on her to help me every day.

To my best Friend Josh, thank you for your years of support. Josh is now the COO of my largest and most successful company, but he is much more than a business associate. Josh has always been there for me when I needed someone and has been like a brother to me for many years. Part of the reason I had time to write this book is because I can depend on Josh to run my businesses when I am unable to devote my time to them. He is not only a great colleague, but also a wonderful friend.

In memoriam to Dr. Hobson Brock, who taught me about selflessness and the importance of giving back. Even though he is gone, Dr. Brock remains an inspirational part of my life, in my charitable work, and in writing this book.

Lastly, I must mention Justin Khalaf, a good friend who convinced me that I had the ability to share my knowledge with others and change their lives. As much as I changed Justin's life, he also changed mine. He showed me that faith in God pulls you through any difficult time in life. I am truly blessed to have such

Acknowledgements

a wonderful friend.

I would like to thank and acknowledge all those who have supported me and believed in me throughout the years, and to all of my students past, present and future. I would also like to thank Wayne and Jacquie at Same Page Press for helping me find my voice and put pen to paper.

THE HIDDEN MILLIONAIRE

Introduction

Birth of a Philosophy

When I started my first business, I was a kid who happened to have a passion for baseball cards. My ambition was not to become wealthy or to reinvent the baseball card industry: I was simply a boy having fun with my hobby and seeking ways to finance it. I did not even think of it as a business. It was merely a way to subsidize my passion. It has been said that when you work at something you love, it's not work at all. Because I was having fun, steadily increasing my collection and making money, this never felt like work to me. The more money I made with my hobby, the more I could spend on my hobby. Hence, my boyhood experience proved to be a life-defining moment.

I cannot honestly say that all of my business ventures have been successful without involving some hard work; in fact, they have all required considerable investments of time and energy. I can say that whether I'm selling baseball cards or running sophisticated businesses that generate millions in revenue, everything I have attempted to do has been infused with tremendous momentum simply because of my passion for creating something new and seeing it through to its logical conclusion. The acts of creation, exploring new ideas and areas, and testing my abilities are thrilling to me. If you find

Introduction

that you are person inspired by similar feelings then perhaps you have the initiative, drive and energy to become
an entrepreneur yourself.

"Entrepreneur"—What It Means to Me

Many people in the business world call themselves
entrepreneurs. Some of them are ethical; some are not.
Some are outright charlatans whose business skills are
defined by their abilities to separate hardworking people
from their money. You can call yourself an entrepreneur,
but if your motives are cheating others and/or acquiring
successful companies and liquidating them just to generate personal wealth, then as far as I'm concerned, you are
not an entrepreneur. I personally reserve that title for
people who create success through their own ideas,
initiatives and foresight. To me, turning other people's
money into your money does not really qualify as entrepreneurial.

My success is not based on traditional business
training, the manipulation of others or blindly lucking
into money but on principles I learned, often by accident
and mostly through perseverance. In looking back on my
early experiences in business, I realized that I had
applied the same principles to each of these early
endeavors. Consequently, I began strategically applying
these principles to each new and successive endeavor
and miraculously my career took off like a shot!
In those early years when I was green and the furthest

Introduction

thing from savvy, I was feeling my way through the marketing and business world. It is my hope that you will be inspired by my story, learn and apply my formula for success and avoid this step.

As an adult, when I started my first business, I went from having no money to generating millions of dollars. As you will soon discover, you can do the same thing at home with nothing more than a computer, an Internet connection, and a little motivation and innovation. All that is required is passion and a little intestinal fortitude.

Yes! There Really Is a Formula for Success

So, is there really a formula for success that anyone can follow? Absolutely! Throughout this book, my Principles for Entrepreneurship are outlined and can be utilized by anyone willing to learn and apply them. This formula for success also includes prerequisites that are applicable to almost every endeavor you will ever embark upon in your life. Hard work and perseverance are the key elements. No matter how brilliant your plan is no idea can be realized without good, old-fashioned hard work and perseverance.

It was Thomas Edison, one of the most brilliant inventors America has ever produced, who said: "Genius is one percent inspiration and ninety-nine percent perspiration." There will always be innovative thinkers, entrepreneurs and industry mavericks, but it's those few

Introduction

who combine good ideas with a great work ethic who pave their own way. Rather than following the accepted path, they discover their own road to success. Traveling down this road will certainly involve effort. No matter how inventive, there is no formula for success that will eliminate the need for hard work. Without effort, even the best ideas are just theories, and theories are a dime a dozen.

You Have Heard It All Before but...

While my story may appear to be similar to others you have heard, there is a distinct difference: It's all true. Too many self-proclaimed "entrepreneurs" sell hype, not facts, to the masses. I distinguish myself from them by honestly providing people with solid, tangible business principles that actually enable them to achieve some level of financial success. Others profess to have the secrets to earning extraordinary wealth and they sell their get-rich-quick books and programs aggressively and unscrupulously. It is not my goal to mislead you with false bravado but to teach you exactly how to maximize every business opportunity by approaching each one well prepared, focused and motivated. Only then is success defined as being on your terms and momentum determined by your level of commitment, not by an arbitrary goal promised by someone hoping to sell you on vague proclamations.

This book will outline simply and concisely what it

Introduction

is you need to know and do in order to realize success as an entrepreneur. I can't promise that you will become a millionaire, but I can promise that you will learn the principles of entrepreneurship, how to adopt the necessary mindset and retain a proper understanding of the process. These lessons will help you create opportunities for yourself that will ultimately provide you with an avenue to success.

If you get nothing more from reading this book than the concept of these principles, and the realization that life is better when you focus your attention and energies on the things that give you purpose, pleasure and enhance the lives of those around you, then congratulations. You're ahead of the game. If it just so happens that in that pursuit you end up being a huge success in business, well, so much the better.

Let's get started...

Anthony Morrison

THE HIDDEN MILLIONAIRE

Chapter One
The Entrepreneurial Mindset

I often tell people that entrepreneurial success is something anyone can obtain if they have the right mindset. Successful entrepreneurs are positive thinkers who consistently maintain their optimism even under stress and, as a result, they have a confidence about them that others can see immediately. We see these people as having "a gift" and assume it's innate, and can't be learned or taught.

It's true that some people are born with an ability to "think" like an entrepreneur, and they do have a definite advantage, but this way of thinking *can* be learned. I teach it every day in my seminars. It's simply a matter of following established principles and applying them to every endeavor. Anyone can be taught to think like an entrepreneur, and whether you're born with it or acquire it, once you have the right mindset and master the basic principles I will provide you with, success is just steps away.

I know that my ideas work because I've personally seen them work, and I've seen lives changed in the process. Whether you're driven by entrepreneurial spirit or by a desire to improve your existing life and work situations, these principles are applicable to life in general.

The Entrepreneurial Mindset

The opportunity to share my experience and knowledge along with my passion to inspire others is what motivated me to write this book.

Find Your Passion

When I started out in business, it was not my intention to become a success guru: My goal was to take all the things that I truly cared about and make them self-sustaining.

Money has never been the ultimate goal or inspiration for me. In fact, I just do what I love to do and money seems to come to me by accident. To me, money as an object is useless except for what it represents. It's only how money is earned and used that determines the measure of its value. Money, as a goal unto itself, will never motivate you the way passion for your endeavor will. Nothing inspires action more than pure passion. To me, when passion is a catalyst to earning more money, it's the ultimate example of success.

I view my business endeavors in very much the same way an artist views a painting, a composer views a symphony, or a scientist views his discovery. Being an entrepreneur provides me with an opportunity to create something every day. My success puts me in a position to give back generously, purposefully and in ways that make a difference in other people's lives.

The Entrepreneurial Mindset

The Entrepreneurial Equation:
Personality Times Five Equals...

I have established that whatever your goals may be, success requires passion and positive thinking, but these factors are only part of the equation when developing the entrepreneurial mindset. There are five additional personality components that are critical to entrepreneurial thinking. They are: **Knowledge, Motivation, Confidence, Strategies** and **Resourcefulness.**

Remember, the difference between a successful person and an unsuccessful person is how they each react during difficult times. Successful people always think positively and are motivated to succeed and better themselves. All successful entrepreneurs have confidence in themselves and a motivation to succeed.

The following five components have been critical to the success of every endeavor I've embarked upon throughout my life. We will examine each of these factors more closely, and how they apply to each of my business ventures, throughout this book.

Knowledge: Knowledge is the *key* to all success. Let's just say it's virtually impossible to succeed at something you don't understand or to master anything you know little about. It's like being blind, deaf, mute and

The Entrepreneurial Mindset

completely naked while trying to walk through a mine-field. There is no better defense than preparing yourself for every eventuality, and only an informed individual has that capacity. Knowledge helps you determine the benefits and pitfalls of every situation. It prevents mistakes from being made and mishaps from occurring. Knowledge also gives you confidence when making decisions and in dealing with peers and rivals within your chosen industry. Knowledge is power. Therefore, it's best to gather as much information as you possibly can about a business before you venture into it.

Confidence: True personal confidence, which is not to be confused with arrogance or misplaced confidence, comes from being secure with yourself and in your abilities. The more knowledge you have in your particular area of expertise, the more confident you are when speaking about it to others. The same principles apply to the entrepreneur. If you know your business well, you will feel secure and confident in your abilities to make it a success. Positive thinking is contagious and your confidence will convey a sense of security to your potential clients, customers and business partners. Security breeds trust, which always makes for successful business relationships.

Motivation: Complacency is the number one killer of entrepreneurial ventures and it's easy to

The Entrepreneurial Mindset

become complacent when things are going well. Motivation fuels success. The more inspired you are to achieve, the more you will continue pushing yourself towards success. Staying focused and motivated is critical to your survival as an entrepreneur and the compulsion to succeed is what will separate the modest achievers from the true innovators and titans of the business world.

Strategies: It's important to form strategies for success in every business you start. Having a good plan is like plotting a treasure map. The steps that point you to the *Big X of Success* should identify benchmarks for achievement along the way and include a process for evaluating your progress. Success will come if your plan is executed correctly—and with your map in hand and strategies in place, you will recognize your achievements when you reach them.

Resourcefulness: Entrepreneurs are resourceful and tenacious. They do not accept "no" for an answer. Entrepreneurs see "no" as a motivator, not as a deterrent. "No" is not a definitive answer to an entrepreneur. When there's an obstacle between them and something they need, they find a way around it. To an entrepreneur, a "no" from a conventional businessperson really means: "There's a better, more convenient and less expensive solution that you can offer me."

The Entrepreneurial Mindset

Entrepreneurs are determined in their resolve to reach a reasonable compromise. Resourcefulness is not to be confused with stubbornness. That implies refusal to accept an answer regardless of the reality of the situation. That's why when there is an alternate route to a successful outcome, an entrepreneur will find it rather than accept defeat.

We are all innately aware of some of these principles. I know that I was initially because I utilized them without even realizing it. Nevertheless, even if you're not in touch with your inner entrepreneur, you can learn these principles and apply them as needed. This is the first **Principle of Entrepreneurship: Develop an Entrepreneurial Mindset.** Remember: Knowledge is power and positive thinking is contagious. Now that you have the map, you have taken the first step towards developing the mindset that will lead you toward success.

Chapter Two
Business as Pleasure

I was born in Jackson, Mississippi, on December 24, 1982, to Roger and Sheila Morrison, two very loving people who provided a wonderful, stable and nurturing home environment. They were, and still are, such a vital and important part of my life. I am the eldest of their three children; my brother Adrian is in the middle and my sister Brittain is the baby.

We lived in Jackson until I was thirteen before moving to the town of Madison. Moving there was an inspiration. To this day, I've yet to see a town as pleasant or a community as close-knit as Madison. Nestled in the rolling hills of central Mississippi, Madison is ten minutes from Jackson, a city with modern urban streetscapes and crime. In contrast, Madison is designed with suburban charm and family values in mind.

In the interest of maintaining the integrity of its visually quaint vistas, big box stores are required to modify their signs to be more aesthetically pleasing to the eye and the use of billboards is prohibited. There was not much crime in Madison because the police were so proactive about enforcing the laws; in fact, to this day, the town boasts the lowest crime rate overall compared to the rest of the United States. I grew up in the ideal hometown. If I hadn't experienced living there, I would've thought such places only existed in movies.

A Charmed Life

My childhood was unconventional in many ways. For example, I did not attend public school. I went to Madison Ridgeland Academy, a private school in town that had a curriculum that appealed to my mom. I was there from kindergarten through 12th grade and was one of only 38 students in my class. These same kids were in my class each year so there was a certain intimacy among the students. Regardless, I always had interests apart from the mainstream. I was never a partier, and I never joined in any activity just to be "cool" or to be part of the in-crowd. I was not an outcast but I was shy, and I purposely lived by my own design, never worrying about fitting in or being popular. Even as a teen I could see beyond the temporary culture of high school, knowing that in a few years, clique mentality and the status that came with being on the football team would be meaningless.

My family was very secure financially, which took a lot of pressure off the daily family dynamic. Never having to worry about money made everyone more relaxed. Having come from rough backgrounds, my parents made certain we would never have to face the problems associated with poverty. They never fought in front of us; they made sure we were always cared for, emotionally and financially. We learned how deprivation can be a great motivator from listening to their childhood stories and how they overcame adversity as adults.

My father was a very successful real estate investor. His father had passed away when he was a child and, being the eldest son, my dad worked since he was a teenager to support his mother and siblings. In fact, he continued to support his mother until she passed away.

My mom left home in her teens and went right into the workforce. After we were born, she stayed home, giving us the family life she had never enjoyed, reinforcing our self-esteem, teaching us at every opportunity and showering us with affection. Having no one to go to for advice, my mom constantly read books on child rearing and psychology for guidance. As a result, there was purpose behind every activity and every bit of information she provided us with, but we could not understand the importance of this until we were older.

My parents had made a promise to each other when they decided to have children. Their plan was for us to be healthy, respectful, compassionate and industrious people. My dad always says I was born "talking straight," meaning I always had a purpose and an ability to focus. Because of this, my mother relied on me to help care for my brother and sister, but she always taught me to care for myself by encouraging me to make my own decisions. From an early age, we learned to think for ourselves.

My parents treated us very well as children and, believe me, we knew it but never developed a sense of entitlement or a feeling that we were any different or better than other people. I remember that when remote-control electric cars became popular, my friends all received them for Christmas. My brother and I got the entire line, but my mother also taught us to give back. During the holidays, the local mall set up a Christmas tree decorated with hundreds of angels. Each angel had a name and represented an underprivileged child. My mom would have us pick angels off the tree and we would go shopping for gifts for each one of those kids. My parents did not want us to enjoy our lives without also having compassion for those less fortunate.

As I mentioned above, my parents kept my brother, sister and me involved in activities they knew would develop our self-esteem. My father knew how important self-esteem and confidence are in business and in life so, to boost ours, we regularly participated in beauty pageants beginning at twelve months old until we were about five or six. When I was two, I won Tiny Tot of Mississippi and went on to win more than fifty trophies throughout my pageant career. I know some people think beauty pageants are a silly activity, but I think building confidence at a young age is important, and I believe participating in the pageants helped me build confidence in myself.

As we each turned five, my parents enrolled us in karate classes. Karate is a sport that helps build determination and discipline, both of which are requisites for success in business. I attended many karate tournaments over the course of the next few years, winning many awards by the time I was eight years old. For those who don't know anything about martial arts, self-defense is the primary objective, but instilling good habits and confidence are also essential components. To this day, I train in karate since the lessons it imparts remain important in many areas of my life.

I realize that growing up in the United States in an upper-middle-class family has advantages. Achieving success is less challenging when you've had a good education and a loving, stable home life and my beginnings certainly don't set the stage for a rags-to-riches tale. In retrospect, my childhood was idyllic and empowering, but there's more to success than just being born into the right circumstances, as I'll explain, because even the most idyllic life can be upended by disaster.

The Young Entrepreneur

I first demonstrated my tenacious nature at age seven when I decided that we really needed a Jacuzzi in our backyard. I had friends who owned hot tubs and,

Business as Pleasure

for some reason, I wanted one. I asked my parents and my mother's response was, "If you want one so badly, why don't you work for the money and buy one?" At seven years old, I didn't even know what work *meant* but Mom, in her wisdom, explained what work involved and said that if I wanted something badly enough, I would find a way to get it. By doing this, my mother taught me how to go get what I wanted at a very young age.

Once it had been explained to me, I didn't mind the idea of working at all, so I thought about it and came up with a great idea. I decided I would sell candy to earn the money for the Jacuzzi. I immediately went to Sam's Club, bought boxes of chocolate bars and began going door-to-door to sell them. My mom was completely astonished that I was actually selling candy bars in order to buy a hot tub. I convinced my brother and sister to get involved, too, by offering to pay them for their help so that I could raise the money faster. For three weeks, we sold candy throughout my neighborhood and in the surrounding community until, eventually, we earned enough money to buy that Jacuzzi.

I didn't know it then but this proved to be a very important life lesson. I realized that what my mother said was true: If I wanted something badly enough, I actually could find a way to get it.

A year or so later, I decided I wanted to buy my dad a motorcycle for Christmas. My dad is the kind of person who always gives so much but will never buy anything for himself. At the time, his brother and several of his friends had motorcycles, and I had overheard him mentioning to my mom that he loved the idea of being able to ride with my uncle on the weekends. Inspired, I immediately turned to what I knew would work: selling candy. I returned to Sam's Club, purchased boxes and boxes of candy and once again began selling it with the help of my siblings. At eight years old, I was able to earn more than $2,000 in a few short weeks and buy my dad a Honda Shadow motorcycle that he still has to this day.

Batter Up!

Those early endeavors were fundraisers with a specific objective in mind. My next business had broader applications and began as a way to finance an activity I enjoyed.

Like many boys, I loved everything that had to do with baseball and in my early teens, I began collecting baseball cards. I had quite the collection and eventually my healthy enthusiasm became an obsession. You know that you have officially crossed the line from hobby to obsession when collecting graduates from simple accumulation to seeking and buying specific and often hard-to-find cards.

When we lived in Jackson, my brother and I shared a bedroom. Once we moved to Madison, I had my own bedroom for the first time, which gave me the

Business as Pleasure

privacy and space I needed to explore the world without having someone looking over my shoulder. Creativity requires space to flourish. We all require a certain amount of privacy to allow our imaginations to soar. At that age, having my own space was very liberating because I was beginning to develop my own identity apart from my immediate family.

When I wasn't busy studying or playing baseball, I would spend most of my spare time on my computer. At that time, most other typical thirteen-year-old kids that I knew would spend their time playing games on their computers, but not me. Even at that age, I saw the computer and the Internet as a way to earn money. I was fortunate to own a computer and be active online when the Internet was first being widely used by the public, and I frequently used AOL Instant Messenger to talk with other collectors and swap cards.

I also loved chatting with friends and reading stock quotes, but what I enjoyed most of all was networking. With IM, I was able to communicate with millions of people all over the world, all of whom were essentially strangers. Thanks to the Internet, I was able to extend my network beyond my circle of acquaintances and immediate geographical area. I was talking with collectors from all over and buying cards I would not necessarily find in my local baseball card store. I was also buying cards I couldn't normally afford, but because I was making a profit with my sales, I could justify spending what otherwise would have

Business as Pleasure

been a lot of money. While my parents were very generous, they had their principles and if I was going to spend $150 on a single baseball card, I was responsible for coming up with that kind of money myself.

I soon realized I could purchase boxes of baseball cards on the Internet even more cheaply than our local stores were paying the manufacturers for them, so I began supplying the baseball card stores in town with their inventory. At thirteen years old, I was making between $200 and $500 a month just selling baseball cards. This lasted until storeowners discovered the Internet, which ended up putting me out of the card supply business, but that was not my only avenue for sales.

I had discovered that I could also sell the baseball cards I purchased online at trade shows in my area. From the first time my father took me to a show, I knew I could succeed in that environment. The other vendors were older men, mostly retired, but they didn't intimidate me. The fact that I was a kid made me an instant draw at the shows because most of the collectors were kids around my age. I wasn't just selling to the demographic—I *was* the demographic. Because of this, the kids felt more comfortable around me than they did around adults, and I certainly didn't shy away from the attention.

We would participate in as many as five local trade shows a year. I would set up a professional booth with the cards displayed under Plexiglas. A retail space at card shows costs money, so I was always aware of how much I needed to make to cover expenses and break even. Of course, I generally did much better than breaking even. To draw potential customers, I devised a dice game that gave cards as rewards—an incentive that many vendors use today. While most kids my age saw baseball cards strictly as a hobby, I had ventured into outside sales and had succeeded.

New Ideas Are All Around You

Back then, I wasn't getting rich from my baseball card hobby but I was earning good money for a thirteen-year old. I wasn't interested in becoming wealthy; I was interested in finding ways to finance the purchase of more baseball cards. The card shows were also an opportunity to participate and operate in the adult world. Nothing builds a youngster's self-esteem like adult interaction on a peer level. I was simultaneously learning how to **strategize**, using the Internet for research. The Internet provided me with instant access to updated information on card trends, such as what cards were most sought after and how prices had changed.

Everyone develops strategies in life. Even a person who holds up a convenience store has a strategy. It's important to have both long- and short-term goals identified and recognize avenues for achieving them. How you develop strategies determines whether

Business as Pleasure

they will be successful.

The baseball card shows also taught me that it builds confidence when others approach you as an authority in your field. I quickly realized that along with knowledge came prestige and authority, and the information I needed to become an authority was readily available. It simply required the motivation to find it.

I realized this in retrospect, of course, but it was through buying and selling baseball cards that I discovered my first **Principle of Entrepreneurship: New Ideas Are All Around You.** Things you're passionate about provide the best businesses ideas, especially hobbies, because your knowledge and enthusiasm for the subject are better **motivators** than money. I knew the baseball card industry and the customer base because I *was* the customer base. Consequently, I had greater success than the adult dealers who, while understanding the principles of commerce, lacked my understanding and dedication.

My hobbies have often become my businesses because each endeavor begins with the idea of enhancing something I already enjoy doing. I think it goes back to the adage that one must do in life what one enjoys in order to succeed. I have lived my entire life by that creed because I truly believe that if you do what you love, the return is by far greater than anything you'll do purely for money.

I also accidentally discovered that the

Business as Pleasure

Internet gave me the forum to do just that, and that would prove to have far larger implications than the selling of baseball cards.

Chapter Three
Being Aggressive Pays

My second business endeavor had similarities to the first in that it also reflected my love of baseball. Growing up in Mississippi without a Major League team nearby, our TV access was limited to two clubs: the Atlanta Braves on TBS and the Chicago Cubs on WGN. For the record, I was a Cubs fan and decided, just as I had with collecting baseball cards, that there was money to be made in conjunction with being an ardent fan.

I managed to convince my father to take baseball road trips, accompanied by my brother, my friend Alex, and his father. When I say baseball road trips, I don't mean driving to single games, as most people do. I mean that we would see that the Braves were going to be in Chicago for three games with the Cubs, and go for the weekend.

I realize many fathers would not have been as indulgent as my dad was with me. Because he was working all the time, so much so that he frequently missed family vacations, we didn't get to see each other as much as we would have liked. These road trips were an opportunity for my dad to spend time with his sons, see a few ball games and relax, and we would go prepared for any scenario.

Many kids would go to the ballpark with a baseball or card in hand, hoping that a player would give them an autograph. We would see these kids clustered around the dugouts and in the field boxes, calling to the players. Sometimes the players would respond, but I was not willing to take that chance, so I devised a plan that would take us directly to the source.

The Autograph Diaries

It began with a trip to watch the Braves in spring training in West Palm Beach, Florida, and became a regular season venture. Before a road trip, I would spend hundreds of dollars buying multiple cards of each player, hats, balls and Major League bats. We would literally fill a trailer with this stuff and bring it on the trip with us.

I would make calls in advance, locate the hotel where the team was staying, and we would stay there as well. We would arrive before the players did, greet them in the lobby, and listen attentively as they were assigned room numbers. Then we would stake out the lobby and exits for the weekend. This being the pre-cell phone era, my brother Alex and I would communicate with walkie-talkies. When we spotted a player, we would converge on him in the hotel, eventually asking every player we met for multiple signings. They often

Being Aggressive Pays

accommodated us and many of the players helped us in our quest for other autographs.

We met Braves third baseman Chipper Jones one year during spring training, and coincidentally he happened to be looking for a very specific card: his. Somehow, he didn't have a copy of his own rookie card, but we had it, more than one, so of course we gave it to him. In exchange, Jones signed everything we had with us: dozens of balls, bats and cards.

That was lucky, but obtaining certain autographs took real planning. We made an extra effort to get second baseman Ryne Sandberg's autograph because he was right at the end of his Hall of Fame career. Sandberg was relentlessly dodging the press and autograph seekers, but he was no match for me. I had a sign that read "Ryne Sandberg Drive" that I had purchased at a previous show and I brought it with me to the games that weekend. We even made sure that our seats were close to where the players' families sat and, sure enough, at the final game we recognized Sandberg's wife in the stands. After the game, Alex followed her back to her hotel.

I sat for three hours in the hallway of the hotel where we suspected Ryne Sandberg was staying, waiting to see if he would return. Luckily, we were right. When he saw me sitting in the hall, it was obvious that he wasn't going to sign anything for me so I presented him with the sign bearing his name and he was impressed. I also had in my possession a ball he'd fouled off two nights earlier. Sandberg graciously signed them both then sent me on my way.

Be Friendly, Polite and Aggressive

There was always a chance that players might feel harassed or exploited by such stalker-like behavior, but we were always friendly and polite and, as a result, some of the players would actually watch out for us. After one particular game, Braves center-fielder Andruw Jones offered us a ride back to our hotel and gave us a bat that pitcher Greg Maddux had used during the game. When we asked him to help us, he convinced Maddux to autograph it.

One problem sports memorabilia collectors have is authenticating autographs. Forgeries pollute the market and there are countless stories of clubhouse attendants and batboys being paid to sign player autographs. A certificate of authenticity will usually accompany many autographs. Many of those certificates could probably use a certificate of authenticity themselves, so we always carried a camera in order to authenticate our autographs. The pictures provided a photographic record of me getting a ball or bat signed by the player, and I made sure to include the photo as my own certificate of authenticity when selling the merchandise.

Being Aggressive Pays

The memorabilia business was my first lesson in one of my **Principles of Entrepreneurship: Be Aggressive.** This is how a hobby or interest moves to the next level. It's essential to be aggressive if you're going to succeed in business. After learning this, I applied this principle to every consecutive endeavor. At fourteen, I was still more interested in funding my private fun than I was in making a fortune, but the principle was in place: Aggressively pursue opportunities; refuse to accept "no" for an answer; create strategies that achieve goals; and eliminate the middleman. I saw the kids on the railing at the ballpark hoping for a single signature, and the signed bats at the concession stand. There were even people who would stake out the hotel where the players stayed. I had circumvented each of these methods by being friendly and polite yet aggressive.

My ability to **strategize** enabled us to take these road trips free of out-of-pocket expenses. Selling just two signed balls paid for everything we had purchased in advance. These family outings were a great opportunity to bond and get away from the pressures of everyday life, and finding a way to accomplish this with no overhead made the idea even easier to justify. I was fortunate to have two adults who were willing participants.

The fact that I was **confident** was a definite key to my success. **Knowing** and having an abundance of

Being Aggressive Pays

information about the players and their accommodations in advance made the venture less risky. In selling the memorabilia, I was again both a customer and retailer. I knew what people wanted because I wanted it, too. Once again, being the insider proved invaluable and I had turned a hobby into a moneymaker. I also happen to have a valuable collection of baseball memorabilia, thanks to the pursuit of my obsession, but as a businessman, I was just warming up.

The Accidental Business

Before taking a step forward with my next venture, I had what I call a small accidental business that, despite its size, served to reinforce some of the lessons I was learning.

Many adults in my community were aware that I had a precocious capacity for sales. On a recommendation, my church approached me, asking if I would help them with a fundraiser. The church had been given boxes of Beanie Babies from Kentucky Fried Chicken, which, at the time, were a very profitable collectible. Apparently, KFC had intended to give them away at their franchises and had decided not to, so they donated them to the church. Faced with the task of selling boxes of Beanie Babies, about which I knew nothing, I decided to take the challenge.

Devising a strategy, I sold the Beanie Babies on eBay, to stores at the mall, and even brazenly sold them

Being Aggressive Pays

by the side of the road right in front of our local Toys 'R Us. I sold them all in the space of several weeks, proudly presenting the church with $5,000. I think they were surprised that I had sold them all at a profit and very quickly so as a reward for my efforts, they gave me $2,000.

This experience is an excellent example of how my basic principles work. Knowing absolutely nothing about Beanie Babies could have been cause for worry. Who wants these? Where do I sell them? How much should I ask for them? I could not initially answer these valid and important questions but I didn't let that stand in my way. To me, boxes of Beanie Babies were simply raw material, and I knew that with a little research and effort, I could dispose of them and help my church. Even when faced with an unfamiliar product, having confidence in yourself and your abilities is of utmost importance. I had already learned the strategies to sell successfully and I knew that they applied to any product and situation. In this case, my instincts proved to be correct.

In the hands of an entrepreneur with **knowledge, motivation, confidence, strategies** and **resourcefulness**, Beanie Babies were as viable to sell as baseball cards. With the success of that incidental venture under my belt, I was well on my way to my next obsession: a Ford Mustang.

Chapter Four
Striving for Knowledge

As all parents raising boys will tell you, it's a quick jump from baseball cards to cars and girls and, sure enough, when I turned fifteen, I fell hard...for a 1996 Mustang GT.

The Face That Launched a Thousand...Chats!

I was with my mom when I first saw her. She was a siren! Fire engine red, sleek, sexy and beautiful—and I wanted her. I had originally thought of buying a BMW but they had manual transmissions and I didn't know how to drive a stick shift. But when I saw that perfect Mustang, the fact that it also had a stick shift suddenly became irrelevant. "You should get it if you want it," my mom said, seeing my excitement. Oh, I definitely wanted it.

I asked my dad for his opinion. Being an old-school car guy, he had owned twenty-two cars at one point himself, and he was just as supportive. "I think you should have this car," he confirmed.

When it comes to cars, some parents worry about their kids having a vehicle with a lot of power—that their worst imaginable fears will come true if their children wreck it or injure themselves. My parents trusted my judgment. They liked that I had a powerful car, although they did tell me that if I got a ticket, the car would be sold immediately. That was their stipulation.

"Remember, if a kid pulls up next to you at the light and wants to race, you don't have to prove anything to anyone," my mom reminded me.

With all that in mind, I drove safely. My parents had firmly instilled in me a sense of responsibility, but I suppose it's still a good idea to reinforce it when your kid buys his first muscle car.

When I got my Mustang, I immediately became obsessed with it. Now, some kids become so obsessed with their cars that they end up putting tremendous amounts of money into them. I was no exception; I was determined not only to make my car good, but the best Mustang ever built. There are plenty of ways to modify muscle cars, and I immediately started looking for chrome rims and mufflers online. My mission was to put every possible improvement into that car. I spent hours on the Internet researching where to find the cheapest parts in the country so that I could make her faster, prettier and give her even more muscle, of course.

It wasn't enough *believing* I had the fastest Mustang in the state of Mississippi; I had to *know* it was true, so I started looking for superchargers online as

Striving for Knowledge

well. For you non-gearheads, a supercharger is a compressor that forces more air into the combustion chambers than a conventional engine does. Increased air plus increased gas equals increased power, but superchargers can cost thousands of dollars. It's one thing having your parents pay for your car insurance; it's another to ask them for thousands of dollars for a single car part.

By visiting chat rooms online in pursuit of parts, I gradually became very knowledgeable about superchargers, Mustangs and the auto parts industry in general. Within these chat rooms and message boards, I found hundreds of thousands of Mustang enthusiasts all in one place. It was exactly like the baseball card industry, only now the toys were bigger and selling for more money. This gave me an idea.

I began matching sellers with buyers. I would find a supercharger for sale, contact a person looking for that specific item, and offer to sell them the posted item for $300 over the posted price. This was my fee for the negotiation. When I had both the buyer and seller in agreement of the terms, I would broker the money, sending the payment, minus my cut, on to the seller. I would then have the seller ship the supercharger directly to the buyer. Very often, I never even saw the part, the buyer or the seller but what I did see was the profit.

Every morning before school, I would check

my e-mail to see if I had any new deals to work on, then the second I got home after school I would go right to work locating new superchargers, buyers and sellers. I'm sure that none of my customers knew I was only a teenager, but that's the beauty of the Internet: visual anonymity. If I had tried buying and selling in person, I might have received a much more skeptical reaction from my clients and customers, but online, where expertise can't be affected or influenced by appearance, all people saw was my confidence and knowledge.

Other People's Money

My supercharger endeavor was my introduction to a business principle that's been discussed before and will continue to be acknowledged in every book on entrepreneurship in the future: OPM or Other People's Money. I was generating income by using OPM and financing my Mustang obsession with part of the profit in the process.

I started buying all the used superchargers posted on the majority of the Mustang message boards. Eventually, I cornered most of the online used supercharger market. I was fifteen years old and anyone looking for a used supercharger online had to come to me. Superchargers cost anywhere from $2,000 to $3,000, which was more than I could afford even for my own car, let alone an investment, but I was rolling approximately twenty to thirty of them a year, without investing a single penny, and I never once reached into my wallet. In the process of buying and selling super-chargers, I was able to turn my 200 hp Mustang GT into an 800 hp racecar, the ostensible reason for the entire venture. All this happened through the power of the Internet—and I didn't even have a job.

During this time, I chatted online with a man named Charles Warren from Lubbock, Texas. Charles was a car enthusiast and mechanic. When I needed work done on my car, Charles agreed to drive to Mississippi and do the job. Of course, my parents were not thrilled at the idea of having this stranger in their home, but Charles was a nice guy in spite of his appear-ance. With his messed-up hair and his Sonic jacket, he was just a few years older than me, and we got along great. He would come to play a much larger role in my life as the years went on, but our initial meeting in cyberspace was another lesson in the power of the Internet. It brings together people of common interests from different areas who otherwise may have never connected. I didn't know Charles from Adam before he arrived, but by the time he left I felt that I had made a new friend for life.

When I began selling car parts online, I under-stood the market because I *was* my target customer. Again, a hobby had quickly become a business, not with the goal of making money, but in the pursuit of something that I enjoyed doing. I wasturning a profit on sales by merely being the middleman, matching prospective buyers with prospective sellers, and often doing nothing more than negotiating online and handling the money. I didn't even own the part, and I was turning a profit!

I continued with my used supercharger business for three years, dumping a lot of the money I earned into modifying my Mustang. Some people would say that was foolish on my part but what the heck! I wasa kid who didn't really *have* any expenses. That experience proved to be valuable regardless because I learned through implementation that **knowing** how a business works is just as important as having a product or service that others want.

This was an early lesson in yet another **Principle of Entrepreneurship: Strive to Acquire Knowledge**. Knowledge is everything in business, and an entrepreneur should always strive to acquire more. Be an expert in your field and if you're intelligent enough to grasp the concept of one industry, you can always teach yourself how another industry works. The ability to learn and apply that knowledge transcends businesses. With that in mind, you can start additional businesses, as the model is infinite in its applications.

My newly acquired understanding of the online auto parts industry, coupled with my **motivation** to succeed, would eventually lead to my first serious business venture. By this time, I had already established my template for entrepreneurial success without even knowing it.

Striving for Knowledge

A Sudden Change in Plans

By the time I was eighteen, I had been selling superchargers for three years, and there was nothing left to modify on my Mustang. Though I was still making money, baseball was calling to me once again.

I was in my senior year of high school and I began playing baseball for the school team for the first time in years. I had declined to play for the school team before because the coach and I hadn't seen eye-to-eye but I participated in recreational leagues that ran throughout the summer months. In my senior year, the school decided to hire a new coach, so I practiced my lefty pitch and came out for the team. Coach Pace was thrilled to see me and wondered where I had been hiding.

I loved being back on the field. Playing baseball was all I had ever wanted to do, and now that I was playing again and really enjoying the experience, I started considering which college I might play baseball for the following year. This left little time for my online sales, which suddenly became a trivial pursuit. Baseball was my priority. But no matter what you have planned for yourself, sometimes the universe has other destinies in mind.

One Friday night after a long practice, I arrived home to find my younger brother in a panic. He could hardly describe what was wrong but by the time he was finished, I had a clear picture of what was happening. Some dangerous boys had been chasing him around Madison in their truck threatening to hurt him. His girlfriend was with him, and he was afraid to take her home because he did not want a confrontation with the troublemakers. Being a protective older brother, I decided I would drive around our neighborhood and scope out the scene. As I suspected, the second I rounded the corner of our street there they were, waiting in their truck for my brother. There were five or six of them and they had obvious intentions of hurting my brother, but he wasn't in the car—I was...and I was a karate expert. Martial arts will not only teach you self-defense, but also how to build your confidence by increasing your ability to remain fearless in situations that may otherwise be troubling. Knowing I was outnumbered didn't bother me in the least. I was there to protect my brother, and the only way these kids were going to hurt him was if I were dead, and that simply was not going to happen.

Once I was out of the car, I had absolutely no trouble dispatching several of them within just a few minutes, but one of them managed to hit me when I wasn't looking. The blow came from an object that still can't be determined to this day, and that blow did serious damage to my face.

I was rushed to the local hospital where I had immediate reconstructive surgery to fix the crushed

Striving for Knowledge

bones in my cheek and eye orbital. As a result of this incident, I now have a permanent piece of plastic that actually holds my eye in place. Doctors also had to work furiously to fix the severed nerve in my face. To this day I have permanent nerve damage that results in other associated pain and headaches.

Because of this injury, I had to sit out the rest of the baseball season senior year. It was tremendously disappointing but I could not risk re-injuring my eye, which at the time was still quite vulnerable. Suddenly, playing baseball in college was no longer important or an option.

I also realized, maybe for the first time, that not every battle is worth fighting, even if you believe you can win. You must choose your battles wisely, and learn to let things go. Perhaps I could have persuaded those boys to stop harassing my brother before I resorted to physical violence, but I didn't even try, and even though I got my licks in, I was ultimately the one who suffered for it. I doubt that any of them had their dreams shattered because of that encounter.

It was a hard lesson to learn, but it forced me to rearrange my priorities. When I was recuperating, I had time to rethink my choices—and while baseball was fun, it didn't seem like something I should be focusing on for the rest of my life. I decided that college should be about getting the best education possible, not about pursuing a dream that might never come true. I needed to focus on something tangible and as I began to heal from my ordeal, that is exactly what I ended up doing.

The Good Doctor

I went to college at nineteen, cut back on my used supercharger sales and quit playing baseball for the first time in my life. I still sold one supercharger or so a month just for spending money, but I mainly focused on school. I passed on going to Ole Miss and Mississippi State, where I'd hoped to play baseball, choosing instead to attend Mississippi College and to major in Pre-Medical Biology. After my hospital experience and convalescence, I made the decision to go to medical school and become a doctor.

My father had always encouraged me to pursue medicine. He housed many young doctors in the apartment complex that he owned across the street from the hospital, and I think he realized I had the discipline and intellectual curiosity to make a good doctor.

I had always found the idea very intriguing. I was also greatly influenced by one of my dad's friends, Dr. Hobson Brock, who happened to be my pediatrician and like a second father to me. He was in his seventies, with no thought of retiring, when he passed away. Dedicated to his patients and his clinic for underprivileged kids to the very end, Dr. Brock was selfless and willing to help others in any way possible. Most people retire and enjoy the rest of their lives relaxing, but Dr. Brock enjoyed helping people most, and that's why he

Striving for Knowledge

continued to work until the day he died. He had always said that he would rather die than lose his ability to work and I suppose that's why he died in the parking lot of his office after putting in a long day. I had so much respect for him and his passion for helping others that I found myself wanting to feel that way about my own life and work, and suddenly a career in medicine seemed like the logical path for me to follow.

I was the first Morrison to attend college, which was a proud moment for my parents. Here I was, earning the opportunity to do something they had only dreamed of for themselves. Both extremely intelligent people who are constantly educating themselves, my parents missed the opportunity to attend college because circumstances pushed them into the workforce at young ages. In spite of this, they are two of the smartest, well-informed people I know. Let's face it: We all know college graduates who act as though they've never learned a thing in their lives and I'd bet that my mom has read more books than most of them.

Focusing on pre-med was time-consuming, so playing on the Internet was something I didn't have much time for, and my Mustang was as good as it was going to get. I went off to college with the goal of becoming a doctor foremost in my mind, but life had a few more surprises in store for me.

Chapter Five
The Fearlessness of Success

U pon turning sixty-five, my dad retired, deciding it was his time to kick back and rest after caring for others for nearly fifty years. During the course of his career, he had owned everything from hotels and condominiums to car dealerships, banks, apartments and more. He'd made millions of dollars in real estate and upon retirement, he decided to invest most of his money in the stock market. At that time, banks were paying very low interest rates and investors were getting better returns on stocks than on bank holdings, so it was a reasonably safe venture. In spite of having me in college and my brother and sister not far behind, he had no financial worries.

The WorldCom Disaster

I was a junior in college when my dad put most of his money into WorldCom. At the time, WorldCom was the world's second largest long distance carrier after AT&T, and had recently merged with another large carrier, MCI. My dad was convinced WorldCom was safe not because it was huge and telecommunications was a thriving industry, but because WorldCom had its headquarters in Clinton, just minutes from where we lived. "I feel comfortable investing in WorldCom," he told me. "I can put my hands on it, I can see it, and I can stand inside the building." He never expected it would ultimately fail.

For three years, WorldCom executives had been using fraudulent accounting methods to mask the company's declining financial condition by painting a false picture of financial growth and profitability to prop up the price of WorldCom's stock. When WorldCom's accountants uncovered $3.8 billion and alerted the company's auditors, they fired the executives and the Securities and Exchange Commission launched an investigation. In the end, they estimated that the company's assets had been inflated by around $11 billion, resulting in the company having to file for Chapter 11 bankruptcy. When the company emerged from bankruptcy that year, it had $5.7 billion in debt and $6 billion in cash, with half of the cash assigned to pay various claims and settlements. Previous bondholders were paid 35.7 cents on the dollar in bonds and stock in the new MCI, but the previous stockholders' shares were valueless.

I remember the day Dad broke the news to me on a family vacation in Destin, Florida. I was standing in our condo looking out at the ocean and the beach, watching people having a wonderful time enjoying life just as I was receiving the news that was about to destroy our lives.

The Fearlessness of Success

I had always told Dad not to hold stocks overnight because you have no control over the information released once the stock market is closed. Typically, we did just that; we bought and sold stocks every day as day traders, but we were never long-term investors. However, Dad felt very secure with his WorldCom holdings, and for that reason made the long-term investment in the company.

When the news broke publicly about the accounting scandal, trading of stock was prohibited. My dad was pensive, but his hands were tied, and when the announcement of the stock devaluing came, there was nothing anyone could do about it. In the space of twenty-four hours, my father lost nearly everything he'd spent fifty years working to earn.

Stepping Up to the Plate

The loss of all of my father's money in the WorldCom collapse jeopardized everyone's future. My parents, who had never before worried about money, were almost broke. Now facing bankruptcy and having to sell our house, they had no money to pay my college tuition. Even the smallest bills suddenly became challenges. Everyone says money can't buy happiness, but I know from experience that the lack of money can make you very unhappy.

My father had never failed to provide for his family before, so for him it wasn't only a financial crisis, it had also shattered his confidence. I'd never heard my parents fight before, but now there were raised voices and accusations as tension mounted throughout the house. While loss makes everyone remorseful, uncertainty makes everyone anxious, and the anxiety in our house was palpable. What would happen to our family now?

I'd never seen my father like this before. He'd always been confident, but now he was visibly shaken, depressed, and angry with himself, even though WorldCom's bankruptcy wasn't his fault. There was no way he could have prevented the disaster, but he blamed himself regardless. He took action immediately, of course, and began looking for a job, but no one would hire him. It didn't matter that he had accomplished so much in his life because, now, all the companies saw was a man in his sixties who hadn't gone to college.

People had leaned on and relied upon my dad his entire life. He'd always supported his mother and she and my uncle had lived in his various apartment buildings rent-free for years. He had taken care of us as well and now when he was down on his luck, there was no one for him to lean on. This defeat had turned someone I saw as strong, secure and successful into a broken man. We tried to cheer him up and motivate him, but nothing we said would shake him from his gloom.

I tried many times to talk to him and remind him that he was once a multi-millionaire in the real estate market, and that he could do it again. His response was always the same, "It takes money to make money, and we have none now." In his mind, this presented an insurmountable hurdle between him and his abilities to succeed. There was just no money to get started. He felt hopeless, and his despair was beginning to weigh heavily on me, not only because I knew we were going to lose so many things that we'd been accustomed to having, but because my dad just wasn't the same.

The money in the bank was quickly dwindling down...my education, Adrian and Brittain's educations, and everyone's futures were now at stake. At some point, someone had to do something to generate an income. I thought that maybe if we all helped, we would somehow be able to sustain our family. I began brainstorming...what could I do to make money that did not require any upfront investment? I could not take just lying in my bed every night worrying and wondering. I had to do something immediately.

One night as I was studying for a chemistry test, it hit me. I could save my dad and the rest of my family from bankruptcy by taking on the burden of making money myself while still going to school. I could buy and sell Mustang parts online. I knew the parts, I knew the industry, and I knew where to find the people. The only thing I didn't know is how to run a real business. I was so excited I called my dad immediately to let him know what I was going to do. To my complete dismay, he shot it down. "It will require an investment, and it might not work," he said. "I don't think it's a good idea. It will take away from your studying time." Although my dad's decision upset me, I continued to pitch the idea to him.

Every night before I went to bed, I would call to check in with him and just tell him I loved him. I'd been saying goodnight to him like this since I was four years old, and going to college had not changed that tradition. Now during our nightly calls, I would discuss our financial situation and beg him to let me start this business to help our family. It had been six months since the WorldCom bankruptcy and nothing had changed accept that money was becoming scarcer every day. Selling Mustang parts online might not have been the entire answer to our problems, but it was certainly better than doing nothing.

The Cool Blue Solution

For the first time in my life, I countered my dad's advice and decided I would start my own auto parts business anyway, feeling its success would be the justification for having gone against his wishes. Besides, we were desperate. So, in February 2004, I started my first real business. CoolBluePerformance.com, an online retail performance parts store, was born, based on my previous success selling Mustang parts.

I knew it wouldn't be easy because I had no start-up money and no credit, so I borrowed one of my dad's

The Fearlessness of Success

credit cards for my setup costs. He was still one hundred percent against me doing this but he didn't really have any other viable options at that point.

I went to the online message boards, searched and found a site designer named LaTesha Burroughs. She was incredible. I explained my situation and that I needed a site where I could display and sell auto parts for my new company and within a few days, she had finished designing the structure, and the site was live.

The website wasn't the only thing I needed to be successful, though. At the time, the online performance parts industry was saturated with thousands of people selling the same things I was selling. I needed something that would make me stand out, something to make me different, something unique. While brainstorming, I realized the answer was to do something nobody else was doing at the time. I decided the best way to be successful was to stay open and never close, so when I launched my business, my slogan was, "We are open 24 hours a day, 7 days a week, for you to call and place your order." I had thought of the one thing that the large corporations had not even considered. Being on corporate time, other companies closed at 5 p.m. Because I was a college kid with a cell phone, I was on my own time and didn't really have to close unless I wanted to.

I knew there were thousands of people who couldn't order parts during "normal business hours" for many different reasons. The best thing for me to do was to cater to those people, especially since no one else was doing it. I also knew that the Internet is world-wide, and people are on different schedules and in different time zones all over the world. One of my biggest customers ended up being from Australia. How did I get him as a customer? I answered my phone at 3 a.m. when he called.

I bought an 800-number to give the impression of a "corporate" look online, and I added a local number, to which I had the 800-number calls forwarded. That local number was my cell phone. This allowed me to be anywhere and everywhere at any time and still operate my business.

Don't Reinvent the Wheel—Make It Better

I realized the way to be successful is not to reinvent the wheel, but to make the existing wheel better. That's exactly what I was doing in the auto parts industry: something different that would quickly make my business a huge success.

In order to proceed, I needed to get key business components in place quickly. A man named Joe Misiti helped me set up my merchant account and eventually became a permanent part of my professional network as my career progressed. Now I had the phones, the site and a merchant account. I had almost everything I needed to run a successful business...except products. What would I sell?

The Fearlessness of Success

I knew the idea was indefinitely sustainable; if I could get just one company to allow me to sell their products, I could make it work. I had no storefront, no track record and no money for merchandise, but I was determined to convince someone, somewhere, that not letting me sell their products would be the stupidest business decision they ever made.

I contacted UPR Products, and after some negotiation convinced them to allow me to sell their products. I then went back to message boards I had once frequented and announced that I had established a site where Mustang parts were available. Then I sat back, held my breath and waited for the phone to ring...and it did!

In its first month, Cool Blue Performance earned $4,800. It was such a relief, such a joy to know that not only had my idea worked, but it had generated enough money to keep my family afloat! That money covered almost all of our bills and gave everyone hope that things would improve, but it involved some sacrifice.

The constant phone calls at all hours of the night interrupted my sleep. I was still in college and it became increasingly difficult to find time to study and even attend class. I had discovered a working idea but I was also standing on the tip of the iceberg and there was so much more to accomplish if I could just manage to follow it through.

When I started Cool Blue Performance, I never considered that my decision might not work. I knew it

The Fearlessness of Success

had to work in theory, and I made it work in actuality. In this case, OPM wasn't even an issue. I'd spent almost no money. I'd established the site and the product line with persistence and belief in the viability of my idea, and little else. This is another **Principle of Entrepreneurship: Don't Be Afraid to Take Risks.** You must have **confidence** in yourself or no one else ever will, and your confidence will help sell your ideas and products. What will separate successful entrepreneurs from unsuccessful ones are the risks they are willing to take. It's best they be calculated risks, of course, but risks nonetheless. Cool Blue Performance was a risk for me at a time when my family was in a financial crisis, but my family's plight **motivated** me to succeed and I had confidence in my idea's feasibility. I also knew about Mustangs; I had **knowledge** of the industry and was passionate about what I was doing so my venture was a calculated risk.

My idea was now operational, successful and bringing in funds that my family desperately needed to survive. I began to wonder: Where could I take Cool Blue Performance next?

Chapter Six
Starting Small, Thinking Big

In my first month with Cool Blue Performance, I had made $4,800 in profit, which really excited me. With additional effort, I knew I could make CBP not merely profitable but a huge success. But I realized that in order to accomplish this, I had to expand.

Turning the Tables

I was so confident in my ability to sell product that I approached manufacturers as if I were the answer to their prayers. Instead of going through *their* interview process as most potential distributors would, I interviewed them, explaining that I needed to determine if it was worth it for my company to even consider selling their product. This approach caught most manufacturers off guard, placing me in a position of authority and giving me the upper hand.

As I had learned in my earlier ventures, the Internet has great value in preserving anonymity and they had no idea that I was a college student and that my business was in its infancy. They responded to my tone of authority and my confidence, which belied my youth and inexperience in business. This approach

worked. Eventually I persuaded most of the manufacturers to waive their buy-in fees, entitling me to
wholesale prices without having to purchase their
products upfront. Thus, I was able to continue growing
my business without having any money. I talked most
manufacturers into drop shipping everything for me as
well, even if they didn't offer it as an option to their
other distributors. By the time they got off the phone
with me, all they could see were dollar signs.

That initial success was all about having a positive and confident approach. In the hands of
unscrupulous people, such an attitude could lead to
bad business deals but I did not intend to take advantage of anyone. I was already a great businessman—I
just didn't have a record of accomplishment. It was
merely a matter of time and I had no doubts. All I needed was that first manufacturer, an innovative idea and
a relentless desire to succeed.

Giving "Good Phone"—An Essential Tool for Success

I maintained a hectic schedule since being open
24/7 as a sole proprietor meant being available all the
time. Every missed phone call might be a lost sale
opportunity and possible missed repeat sales, so I
had to stay focused in order to stay ahead of my
competition.

Different companies selling the same product or
service on the Internet or in the phone directory can

appear to be very similar. It's difficult to tell one from the other and discern which provides the best services. Often people will buy from the first company that answers the phone because they can't tell the difference between a bad company and a good one.

Because I was the only one answering the phone in the middle of the night or on a Sunday morning, I was intercepting sales calls my competitors had not even considered. Thanks to my open all night policy, I heard from Mustang owners and enthusiasts all over the world, even ones in Australia who were never on the same clock as the American retailers—and they were sure surprised to get a human being on the phone at 4:00 a.m. So while these calls were exhausting, they were also rewarding: I was capturing an untapped part of the market. I realized if I missed any one of those calls for any reason, I was just like all the other companies so I made sure to answer as many as I could. I was hungry. I knew I had discovered my niche and I simply couldn't afford to *not* answer the phone.

This is how I came to notice that this was one of many Internet flaws. It was a problem that I addressed by incorporating my 24/7 strategy. People are skeptical of almost everything they see online because there are so many frauds and swindles throughout the Internet. As I mentioned before, everything looks the same online and there is no way to determine how reputable a company is when all you see is a web page. If the indiscriminate nature of the Internet made it hard to filter out the illegitimate businesses, how could one set oneself apart from all the others? For one thing, people crave human contact and nothing seals the deal like a friendly, helpful voice on the other end of the phone line. Presenting a phone number on my site allowed visitors an opportunity to engage in that vital human contact.

Virtual World versus Real World

Just knowing that they could call and speak to a live person created a sense of security for the customer because they felt that they could call, connect and ask questions. They weren't mired in a maze of e-mails and voice prompts, leaving messages for invisible and unknown people. This accessibility and personalized customer service helped convert visitors into customers, and first-time customers into regular customers. One can always reduce a 24/7 schedule once a business is established but, for starters, nothing impresses a customer like knowing someone is there to answer the phone.

When you promise 24/7 access and you have no store, business is whatever comes to you so I was always sure to carry a pen and pad in my pocket just in case. I took orders while in class, at dinner with my girlfriend and family, even on vacation. I spent many summer days on the beach with a cell phone and laptop because I was always ready at a moment's notice to conduct business.

This took a toll on my personal life. I was unable to have a regular sleeping schedule because of the calls I would get all through the night. I couldn't go to parties because the background noise was unprofessional. I walked out of movies to take calls. I walked out of intensive pre-med classes to take calls. The fact is there was no uninterrupted down time or class time or study time—or even girlfriend time. There was only the vibration of the phone, no matter what else was going on in my life at that time. It was an intrusive and uncomfortable situation and it began to wear on my girlfriend's patience. She didn't understand that this part of my business plan required **dedication** and my complete attention. Any distraction was potentially sabotaging my business.

There are some people who will promise you that an Internet business is an instant money-generating, no-work-required endeavor, but this type of business won't make you millions of dollars while you vacation in Hawaii. It requires your full attention. Just because a business is defined as being Internet-based doesn't mean that the work remains in cyberspace. In some ways, online retail stores *are* just like real brick and mortar stores as far as the enormous personal investment of time and energy involved. Besides answering the phone, I processed the orders, sent out the parts and did the paperwork. Going this route requires a great deal of time and energy.

Starting Small, Thinking Big

The Middleman Factor

Toward the end of my first year in business, I decided that CBP needed to have its own line of product. Because I saw that most people consider manufacturers to be the source, as things were, I was technically a middleman. I did not like the idea of the public's perception of my company being that I was an intermediary or broker so I contracted with a company to manufacture my own CBP products. By putting my company's name on products, I was establishing myself as a direct competitor. Now I had the products I wanted for less cost and no middleman factor confusing my customers.

By the end of that first year, I had done nearly half a million dollars in sales, closing more than 1,300 deals and clearing $76,000. I had accounts with all of the major manufacturers. I was a full-time pre-med student who ran his business part-time from a cell phone and computer, and I still managed to save my family home and my own college education. I wasn't ready to work at CBP full-time, since I still aspired to be a doctor, but I realized that there was a future in this business, and I knew the lessons I was learning would be applicable to other businesses.

Starting Small, Thinking Big

Failure Is NOT an Option

Cool Blue Performance only started small because I had no resources but the goal was always to pursue it to its logical conclusion: to dominate the market, create my own manufactured brand and make the company as large and successful as possible. Even when my resources were small, I was thinking big right from the start, which is another **Principle of Entrepreneurship: Start Small but Think Big.**

If you're starting small with no ambition of becoming larger, or you can see the ceiling of success as soon as you start, you'll remain small. No entrepreneur starts out with restrictions. Set your sights high, use the resources you have, and aim to be the best and the biggest. Never doubt yourself and stay motivated; it's easy to slack off if you're tired, busy, or just not interested. It's inevitable that you will feel frustrated at times, but here is a little known fact: Successful people get frustrated, too, but the difference between them and the people who fail is that they don't allow the frustration to defeat them. Sometimes the beginning requires a lot of work with no return, but you must be persistent and constantly look to the future. Ask yourself: How successful will I be if I keep working at it?

It's easy to fail but if the idea is sound then failure can only result from not pushing hard enough.

Starting Small, Thinking Big

The Internet is not a get-rich-quick portal. Nothing in life is that easy or everyone would be wealthy. Anything you try can be an avenue to success, but it requires work, time and effort to succeed. With Cool Blue Performance, I never doubted whether I could do it or not. Failure was not an option. I knew it would make money; the only question was: how much?

Measure by Deeds, not Dollars

When I realized a profit at the end of my first month, I was satisfied that my idea had real potential. Furthermore, it brought me great joy to realize that I had saved my parents from bankruptcy and simultaneously alleviated my father's feeling of helplessness. I had found a way to pay my parents back for their years of devotion to our family. Being a success in business is a great feeling when you can measure your accomplishments with dollars and cents, but the most wonderful feeling of accomplishment I've ever experienced came from knowing that I was relieving my father from a financial strain when nobody else could.

Helping someone when they are down is a noble gesture. I'm very grateful that my parents, who were always selfless and family-oriented, helped me develop a sense of responsibility and understand the importance of giving to those less fortunate. There is no feeling like the satisfaction that comes from helping someone who has given you everything without ever asking for a thing in return. Where my family was concerned, I did so happily. To think I had never even *seen* a bill before the WorldCom disaster, and now I was in a position to pay them all.

The family dynamics changed the moment I took action. My mom no longer worried and finally slept peacefully; my dad could finally fall asleep at night knowing everything would be all right and my brother and sister's futures were secured as well.

By 2005, CoolBluePerformance.com had become a huge Internet retail website. I was in my final year of college, still studying hard and hoping to finish by the end of the year. I was still operating the business solo, never entirely escaping the stress and the constant calls. I was spending more and more time on the phone and on the computer, talking to customers, taking orders and processing them. Running a successful online business had consumed almost my entire life.

I had alleviated my father's stress and worry and had rescued my family financially. However, how much longer could I go at this pace?

Chapter Seven
Achieving Balance

By the end of senior year in college, I had completely burned myself out. I was studying for the MCAT (Medical College Admission Test) and running Cool Blue Performance at all hours of the day and night. I would literally answer the phone no matter what I was doing. At the time, I had enrolled in a supplemental Kaplan course to prepare for the MCAT eight hours a week and it seemed every minute in between was spent studying or running my business.

CBP was now earning big money and I had rescued my family and my education, but it came at a price. I had no personal life, no free time, no sleep and, after living like this for more than a year, I was becoming increasingly unhappy. Every day I woke up feeling like I carried a 10,000-pound weight on my shoulders, but I had willingly placed it there, and there was no way to pass that responsibility on to someone else. Who but me could run my one-man business?

I wanted to give it up at times but, like the possibility of failure, this was not an option. At some point, I had crossed an invisible line because while I was making enough money to maintain my family, it wasn't enough for me. I felt that I had to continue building

Achieving Balance

CBP and make it as big as I could. I had to not only succeed but also *exceed* every other company's revenue. As tired and overwhelmed as I sometimes felt, I couldn't stop pushing myself to earn more money and build my business.

A Friend for Life

In April of 2005, it was finally time to take the MCAT. Designed to assess problem solving, critical thinking, written analysis and writing skills, in addition to knowledge of scientific concepts and principles, this test was the moment I had been working toward for four years.

The morning of the MCAT, I awoke to another disaster. The phone rang at about 4 a.m. and it was my best friend, Josh, on the other end of the line. He was distraught and in a panic, having just received word that his father had passed away. He was on his way home from Mississippi State University, where he attended college.

I had known Josh since we were kids so when I received the call, I was extremely upset and I had a very tough decision to make. In order to be with Josh and support him through this difficult day, I would have to skip the MCAT exam that I had spent countless hours preparing for. I asked myself what was more important—and I knew I had to be there for Josh. He was my best friend and he had absolutely no family.

Achieving Balance

His father had been his *only* family other than my parents and me. It wasn't even a hard decision to make. There are some things in life more important than work and school. Friendship is certainly one of them, so I decided to skip the MCAT and be there for my friend.

This situation really taught me a lesson about people and the things that are important to them. Sometimes their values seem skewed. Josh was a great athlete in high school; in fact, he was probably one of the best football players in our state. Because of this, he didn't have to pay for tuition, clothes or food. While his dad worked very hard, private school tuitions were out of his budget and this scholarship helped tremendously. As Josh was helping the school win football games, many of the parents who supported our team worked together to make sure that Josh was taken care of. When his father passed away, I expected these same football parents to come together and help him financially. He was in a bind and his father didn't leave him with a life insurance policy, only bills. It dawned on me that when someone loses their value, people seem to stop caring about their well-being. Josh no longer played football, so why would people come forward to help him out?

I decided that I would use the power of the Internet to get donations for Josh. I made some posts on the message boards I frequently visited, and I posted a message on Cool Blue Performance telling Josh's story and explaining his unfortunate situation. As a result, I received quite a bit of money and donations from complete strangers wanting to help Josh. These were not his best friends or people he played sports with in high school. They were just genuine, caring, nice people concerned enough to reach out and help someone in a time of need, and the Internet once again was my gateway to making this happen.

After the funeral, Josh moved into my house and my parents treated him like another one of their kids. Not only was he broke, but he had inherited his father's debt as well, so we all took care of him. Josh is one of those people you meet once in a lifetime. He was determined to make something of himself no matter what life threw at him. I'm proud to say that even with the adversity he faced in life, Josh finished business school, graduating from Mississippi State University, and today he is the COO of the largest and most successful company I've started to date. More on that story later...

The Importance of Balance

It was time to make another tough decision. I could reschedule my exam but assuming I passed the MCAT, there was still no realistic way to attend medical school and operate Cool Blue Performance at the same time. Not if I intended to maintain my physical and

Achieving Balance

mental health, which I had ignored for a year and a half. I knew that the classes in medical school would be even more intensive than in pre-med and some of the tests might require as much as eighty hours or more of studying. Interrupting my studies or cutting out of class to take a call could put me at risk of falling behind. This would be a disadvantage in comparison to my peers, and there was no point in going to medical school if there was even a slight chance I would not actually become a doctor, never mind the fact that I had no life besides school and Cool Blue Performance.

My life had become all work and no play so, at the conclusion of my senior year, I decided to pass on medical school and focus entirely on business and repairing my non-existent social life. I graduated from Mississippi College in December 2005 with a 3.36 GPA.

Being finished with school was a tremendous relief. Even though part of me still aspired to be a doctor, dealing with one full-time occupation after juggling two for the past year and a half felt like such a reprieve. I had succeeded with my business but now I was realizing that I had isolated myself from everyone I cared for. I had very few friends because I simply didn't have time for them. I had dated the same girl for years but even she was growing tired of all the interruptions and my preoccupation with work. Even on Christmas Day, as we opened gifts, I answered the phone.

My success was indisputable, but it was easy to

see that my fixation was ruining the rest of my life. What benefit was there to being a success if I had no time to enjoy it? I eventually lost my girlfriend because my commitment to CBP superseded my commitment to her. It was at this time that I realized another **Principle of Entrepreneurship: Balance Work and Life**. Yes, success requires dedication, but it's essential to know when it's time to stop working and take time for your personal life. Life for me was now shifting into a lower and slower gear, which was good.

With my burden alleviated by the decision to suspend my schooling, I was more determined than ever to succeed, but it would require **resourcefulness** to find a way to balance career success with a normal life. That's when I began to research the subject of marketing financial products on the Internet.

Balance and the Beast

I discovered the benefit of a business such as this was that I wouldn't be required to baby-sit 24/7. It really didn't require my presence at all, unlike a mail-order operation where I was the answering service, shipping department and bookkeeper. With financial products, there is no customer service and no phone time involved, yet I could still turn a good profit. The concept certainly made sense to me, as it was a very simple and easy approach to business online. When I finally decided to move forward with this idea,

Achieving Balance

I contacted LaTesha Burroughs to build my new website. Just as principles of business are applicable to every endeavor, quality people are a resource that I utilize repeatedly and, true to form, LaTesha delivered for me yet again.

After all this, I started CreditCardINC.com in 2005. The key element to earning money with CreditCardInc.com was getting paid commissions from various financial institutions for sending them customers. To succeed, I needed to earn the highest payouts possible. *How could I accomplish this?* I wondered.

Commissions increase as the volume of business increases, so how could I immediately begin earning top-tier commissions without having done any business previously with the company? The answer was simple: Just as I had done in expanding my product lines with Cool Blue Performance, I needed to sell myself, convince the institutions that I was a tremendous resource to them, and the rest of the business would fall into place, which is exactly what I did. Negotiating the top payouts on every offer I promoted gave me the best chance for higher earnings.

Again my confident approach was what got me what I wanted, and what my business needed to be successful. That first month CreditCardINC.com made $1,000, but I knew it was just the beginning, and I was right. Each month since then, profits from that business exceeded the previous month's earnings.

Achieving Balance

Making Things Work

My restlessness had again prompted me to start a new business, but this time because I was out of school my schedule was more relaxed. Oddly, there was still tension at home, although lack of money wasn't the cause. Our newfound source of family income was affecting my dad, and I completely understood his reaction. I could see how it hurt him when Brittain would come to me when she needed money. He had always been the provider. That was his role, but he had become displaced and it was not his fault. My efforts were a selfless pursuit that had saved our home, but at the same time, I knew it wounded him to be dependent on anyone other than himself.

I encouraged him when he became proactive, taking a class offered by AARP about e-mail. This was new territory to him, as it is for many retirees who had thrived in a world without the Internet, so what could this new technology possibly teach them? When he came home, he was eager to show me what he'd learned, particularly since the teacher had told him he knew enough to teach the class. Honestly, though, the class had barely scratched the surface of what he needed to know in order to utilize a computer. I didn't want to embarrass him, so I offered to teach him how to operate computers myself. With that, I had an epiphany.

Achieving Balance

I could free up my schedule and empower my dad by teaching him how to run Cool Blue Performance.

It took me six months to get my dad up to speed, but it was worth it. Before long, he was doing everything I had done to operate CBP. As I stated in the introduction, all you need to be happy in life is love and work, and Dad now had both. Working didn't add stress to his life; on the contrary, it gave him purpose and *removed* stress. This was something I had not anticipated when I first conceived of Cool Blue Performance. Now I was able to give him back the sense of purpose and self-worth that he had lost after the WorldCom failure, and simultaneously help myself in the process.

Through the experience with my dad, I learned that I had the ability to teach others. There is more to teaching than simply sharing knowledge. There is human interaction that requires patience and the ability to convey information in a way that's understandable. Not only did I feel comfortable teaching my dad, I sensed that I was good at it. This was a realization that would have business applications soon enough.

The Power of Perseverance

CreditCardINC.com is now a leading credit card provider on the Internet. We earned more than $500,000 in our first year in business and have

Achieving Balance

generated a steady increase in profits monthly since I started it. In 2005 alone, Cool Blue Performance earned more than $1.2 million in revenue. The business that I had started to save my family was now making us comfortably well off, and my second business was doing remarkably well, and quickly. We could now have everything we once had and more because my two online companies combined had grossed almost two million dollars in a single year.

A benefit of my business equation was that I ran both companies from my home, working in my bedroom on a $2,000 laptop. There were no buildings, loans, mortgages, tenants or overhead to deal with. The Internet had proven to be a fertile ground to launch two businesses, and they'd both succeeded beyond my wildest expectations.

However, the absolute best thing that came from my decision to move back home and focus on my work was that I was able to teach my dad enough about the Internet to work with me. He currently handles 90 percent of Cool Blue Performance business, processing orders, checking e-mail, charging credit cards and shipping products. He'd made millions of dollars in real estate and investing, but he had never touched a computer until he was retired and in his sixties. Today, at nearly seventy years of age, he is running a million-dollar business from a computer that, until recently, he didn't even know how to turn on. That is a fine example of how the power of the human spirit and

Achieving Balance

perseverance can help us overcome any obstacle.

I still find it amusing when my dad calls and tells me to e-mail him things. Just a few years ago, e-mail was a complete mystery to him, and now it's a part of his daily life. He has branched out into an area of business that was once unknown to him and the opportunity has made him a well-rounded person and allowed him to be extremely successful for a second time in his life. There are second and third acts in life if you want them. My dad is proof that no matter what happens, you can start over and come out on top again.

As for me, I managed to have a personal life again but in spite of the free time and the success of my two businesses, I refused to be complacent. If anything, the lack of stress and the dual successes made me even hungrier, and my usual restlessness and inquisitiveness brought me to my next business venture.

Chapter Eight
Business Outside the Internet Box

It would be easy enough to end my story here, and it would still be compelling. After all, I had created a business and operated it in my spare time, and had been so successful with it that I saved my family from financial ruin. It's a great story, one that most people would find inspirational, and I could easily pat myself on the back and quietly slip into a life of semi-retirement now, in my early twenties, but my beginnings are only part of my continuing story.

Once the ball was rolling, I did not intend to rest just because I was successful. I wanted be more successful. I aspired to explore other areas of business and so immediately set out to find new ways to apply my ideas to them.

The Emancipation of Justin

After teaching my father how to operate CBP, I had time on my hands. Both of my businesses were now self-sustaining, and I was looking for my next challenge. Up to this point, each of my businesses had been operating in a virtual medium online, and I always referred to that medium as "the Internet box."

Business Outside the Internet Box

The Internet has its own business rules, laws, and guidelines that are dissimilar from every kind of conventional business that preceded its existence. In many ways, it's like the Wild West and the rustlers are running off with everything that's not nailed down. You might also say the lunatics are running the asylum when it comes to the Internet. Again, maintaining anonymity, for example, is simple when you're in the Internet box, never actually meeting the people you work with on a daily basis.

Up to then, I had yet to engage in anything resembling a conventional business. Probably the closest I had come was when I sold baseball cards at a folding table, but that was about to change.

It turned out that a very dear friend of mine, Justin Khalaf, reached a crossroad in college at the same time I did. Justin and I often studied together because we were both pre-medical majors. When he would come to my apartment to study, he would sometimes become very irritated with me because of all the interruptions.

As you know, at that point in my life, I was completely addicted to the Internet and my computer, so I had a hard time concentrating on anything for more than a few minutes without checking my e-mail, processing orders for my retail site, or answering the phone to take new orders for CBP. It was hard for us to get anything done because I was continuously stopping to operate my business. I was accustomed to the interruptions, because the interruptions to me meant money that my family desperately needed. To Justin, they were just interruptions.

It was hard to ignore my constant preoccupation with business so finally, out of curiosity, Justin inquired about what I was doing and how much money I was earning doing it. He was one of my favorite people in the world and a patient study partner, so in early 2005, I decided I would help Justin make some extra money online. By this time, he was planning to get married and we both knew married life was not cheap. Justin was graduating in May of that year and hoping to attend optometry school the following fall. We both knew that an extra income would be very useful to a newly married, full-time student.

Justin and I began meeting at my apartment for an hour or so each day between classes and study time. I was able to teach him the basic concepts of what the Internet could offer him and the easiest and fastest way to earn money online. I explained in detail the concept of something called affiliate marketing, a web-based marketing practice in which a business rewards one or more affiliates for each visitor or customer brought about by the affiliate's marketing efforts. The theory was the basis for my own CreditCardINC.com, which was making a tremendous profit.

I helped Justin set up a financial services marketing website and hosting account and gave him a brief tutorial on Google, Yahoo and pay-per-click a dvertising. Over the next few months, Justin began trial-and-error testing with his new business, and by the time he graduated from Mississippi College in May 2005, he was earning a few thousand dollars a month. I kept reminding him to spend cautiously, that toys were fun but he had a long life ahead of him and he needed to save. In retrospect, it's funny. Here I was, a 22-year-old kid, telling another 22-year-old kid how to conduct his business, save money and plan for the future.

What did I know about the future or planning? I knew my dad had planned well and that had not turned out as expected, but I was being pragmatic and cautious and looking out for Justin's best interests. The advice seemed sound, even if I didn't have a wealth of experience on which to base it.

Justin was disappointed when he wasn't accepted to optometry school that spring but, like mine, his disappointment was tempered by the possibility of pursuing another opportunity, so he decided to make online affiliate marketing his full-time business and turned all his energies in that direction.

In 2005, Justin earned nearly $18,000 from his affiliate website. Today, Justin is married and earning a full-time income from the same website that I helped him start when we were in college. In 2006, Justin earned more than $300,000 *profit* and was able to build his dream home and pay for it with *cash*. He was also able to buy a new car and take vacations in exotic locations like Hawaii and Cancun.

Business Outside the Internet Box

Even I was curious as to how Justin was able to accomplish so much in so little time. When I asked him, he replied, "I did everything you told me to do." Justin's answer amazed me. He followed my instructions on how to make his business profitable and it worked out really well. He also followed my advice on saving money for the future. Now he and his wife never have to worry about a house payment for the rest of their lives.

I had just pulled my 65-year-old father out of a situation that almost cost our entire family our home. Now this 24-year-old was secure in the fact that he would never have to face such circumstances because he had listened to the advice of a 22-year-old who was just getting his feet wet in the business world.

Such moments remind me of the time my brother, sister and I received our first computers. Upon giving us these incredible gifts, my dad also presented each of us with a picture of a man standing at a fork in the road, pondering which path to take. One path led to happiness and prosperity, the other to sadness and misfortune. Dad hung those pictures over our new computers to remind us that there's a clear choice between the right and wrong paths. That moral reasoning always made sense to me but those paths also represent the safe route and the alternative route. It's like "the road less traveled" in the Robert Frost poem. Justin and I both faced the divergent paths of the conventional career and the daring, and we chose the daring route, never looking back for one minute.

Because he was unable to attend optometry school, Justin faced the same tough choices I myself had faced. In many ways, it's a generational right of passage, having to compete with people of a similar age and similar backgrounds for jobs and careers that don't excite us or present us with opportunities to excel. Justin could very easily have taken the safe route and entered the traditional job market, but he took a chance. The website we established has proven to be not only a source of additional income, but also an invaluable resource in his life.

I'm not sure who gets greater joy from Justin's success, he or I. He's certainly happy, but it literally brings tears to my eyes when I think about his life and how things have changed for him. I am profoundly happy knowing that I taught someone a skill that has changed not only his life, but also the lives of those closest to him forever. Justin is a very philanthropic person who gives back to the church and local foundations. He feels that God has blessed him with success and, in return, makes sure to pay it forward, a principle that is important in business, and one I'll address in a future chapter.

An Interesting Idea

The more I thought about teaching Justin how to start his own online financial services company and my

Business Outside the Internet Box

father how to operate Cool Blue Performance, the more the idea of teaching others stirred my imagination. I realized I was very passionate about sharing information on how to become financially successful and despite my limited experience I was good at it, so that became my next big idea. I decided that I would teach the secrets of success based on my own humble beginnings and experiences.

Being successful on the Internet had brought me a great deal of exposure, especially in my hometown. Every time I ventured out around Madison, people would ask me how they could learn to do what I did. I knew that it was impossible to find the time to teach them individually. I was good but I wasn't Superman! Still, the idea of helping people get started in business, and teaching them how to control their own economic fate, was intriguing. I decided that it would be possible to instruct people in groups but finding those interested in learning and getting them together in one place was a challenge. Then it dawned on me: seminars!

I immediately began brainstorming and educating myself on the seminar industry and what it took to be successful within that world. I started piecing my thoughts together and made lists of the things I would need. First, I needed to have a system built and so, once again, I contacted my resident expert, LaTesha Burroughs, and asked her to work her magic.

I also knew I would need a speaker for my

Business Outside the Internet Box

seminars and a hook that would make my company unique and different from all the others. There are so many seminars offered throughout the business world and because of their similarities (and, in some cases, their seediness), many people shy away from them. I started watching infomercials and attending different kinds of seminars for comparison and noticed a few things they all had in common.

For one thing, most of them were just selling books and ideas on how to make money, but none of them actually put people in business by the time they left the seminar. They were all about selling theories, not tangible plans or solutions. Most had very little to offer as far as practical help and solid ideas. Another thing I noticed was that in most cases, the actual owner of the company, the guru of the entire enterprise, was never there—*never!* They would appear in the infomercial and/or on the cover of the books and accompanying materials, but never at the actual seminars. There were representatives doing the actual lecturing, selling the products and teaching the techniques, but you never saw the actual face of the company at a seminar.

I decided I needed two things to be different in the seminar industry: I needed a program to put people in business before they left my event, and I needed to be there *in person* to teach them how to use my system. Anyone paying good money to be educated deserved more than vague promises. They needed to leave the seminar with a real plan for success. In turn, their success would guarantee my success. Once I recognized these truths, I was ready to move forward.

Thinking Outside the Box

Being a novice in the seminar business, I knew I needed help. I'd never had a business partner or a boss, for that matter, and I'd never even had a mentor. I always did everything on my own, making it up and learning as I went along. My success was a result of my own performance and I liked it that way. Sure, I had all the responsibility, but I also had all the satisfaction and the credit. As I began putting the pieces together to start my seminar company, my parents became nervous. This was my first attempt to step outside of the Internet box, and they knew the real business world wasn't an easy place to navigate.

I was twenty-four, successful beyond all reasonable expectation and had no clue why they were so worried. What was there to be nervous about? I had conducted business with people all over the world. The prospect of tackling the seminar industry didn't intimidate or scare me in the least.

Despite my assurances, my mom was convinced that I needed help. She set up a meeting for me with someone she knew who had been conducting real estate seminars for nearly twenty years. This man, let's just call him Dave, lived in Mississippi and was a speaker for some of the largest seminar companies in the country. My mom knew he had the experience and knowledge to point me in the right direction. I was a novice and I realized that his advice could only help me, if he was even willing to offer it, so I agreed to talk with Dave.

I was disappointed that his staff rebuffed me when I called, but my mother knew his wife and called her on my behalf. "Anthony has a good idea for a seminar," she explained. "Can he spend a few minutes with Dave?"

I was nervous about meeting Dave because he was a multi-millionaire who had worked in the seminar industry for years. He rarely met with anyone about anything, even though people with ideas constantly approached him. Until I presented my idea, I was just another guy off the street to him, but I went to the meeting at my mom's request and decided I would be confident in my approach. I knew that the confidence I had in myself and my idea was just as important as the concept itself.

When I arrived at Dave's office, I realized that I was out of my element. I'd never done anything like this before. Meetings were not a part of my business background. I'd always worked within the anonymous world of the Internet. That anonymity is very reassuring, particularly when you're young and inexperienced in comparison to the people you're dealing with. Dave shook my hand and escorted me to the boardroom, which contained a long conference table. I was thinking how much it looked like Donald Trump's room on *The Apprentice*.

I really was in a state of shock, but the moment he asked me to describe my product and system, I snapped out of it. It didn't matter whom I was talking to or where I was. I knew my system, I knew my idea and I knew what I wanted—and because of that, it was easy for me to present my idea with confidence.

A few hours into the meeting, I could tell things were going well. I was told that typically Dave didn't meet with people for hours, yet I had been there for several already, without being shown the door. Our meeting ended somewhere around 1:00 a.m. that evening. Dave was not only impressed with me, but also with my system and ideas. He wasn't interested in pointing me in the right direction; he wanted to be an integral part of the process, speaking for the company and promoting my system. I walked into the meeting nervous, and I left the meeting with a mentor.

Affiliate Income, Inc.

This meeting with Dave marked the turning point in my business career. I'd made a serious change in my approach to business by allowing myself to have a mentor, someone to help me with my business. It was exciting and strange at the same time because I wasn't accustomed to collaborating, but Dave had knowledge about the industry that would otherwise take me years to learn on my own. Having him on my seminar team was the best thing I could possibly do.

When you operate a business that utilizes employees, it's essential to surround yourself with people who make you work smarter, people you can learn from. Dave certainly fit that bill.

Meanwhile, back at home, my parents were ready to call the police, assuming I'd met with disaster after not showing up for dinner that night. It didn't occur to them that Dave would not only be interested, but would want to bat the idea around with me well into the evening.

That night we agreed to launch a seminar company, which I christened Affiliate Income, Inc. There were many things we needed to address first, however, and they weren't things I was accustomed to dealing with. The first thing Dave wanted to do was test my system. Before he was willing to speak for me and promote my business, he wanted proof that my system worked. Dave and several of his employees sat down with me and I systematically explained what I knew and what I wanted to teach people at my seminars. In that meeting, I literally put Dave and his employees in business, just as I intended to do with the people who attended my seminars.

Dave and his people all made money their first month in business, and he was convinced that I had more than just a theory to sell. My idea was real.

At that point, I had a major decision to make.

Business Outside the Internet Box

For the first time in my career, a business venture was going to require money up front, and it was a substantial financial investment. I was now outside the Internet box where I had previously conducted all my business with low overhead. I discovered that in the real world, businesses need lawyers, accountants, employees and many other things to make it successful, and I was about to get a complete picture of just what was required. I decided to make the investment and move forward with the seminar business.

The first thing we did was charter the corporation. This was the first time I would be operating as a corporation; previously I operated my businesses as a sole proprietor. Once the corporation was established, we had to create all the necessary paperwork for the company. This was the first time I fully understood the concept of lawyers and their fees because I had never in my life hired a lawyer. I needed terms of agreement papers and contracts created for the company, and I needed to design a logo and letterhead.

What I also needed was an office. Dave allowed me to rent a small office in his building so I could get started and I was now operating a traditional brick and mortar business. My Internet businesses were real, of course, but didn't require the same management skills needed to run a business with employees, an office and the hundreds of other things that come with brick and mortar businesses.

I had always dreamed of being corporate. I

remember sitting in my bedroom watching a TV show called *The Big Idea*, seeing CEOs of major corporations on the show and thinking, *One day that will be me... One day I want to be a CEO.*

I didn't realize how easy I'd had it in my Internet box.

My dad ran CBP, and the CreditCardINC.com website practically ran itself, so I was yearning to have important work to do. I was now a CEO running a big company. I had finally achieved that childhood fantasy and was about to realize how much trouble being "the boss" really was.

After establishing my office space, I needed to assemble a team and begin working on the seminar project. I discovered that there are many moving pieces to a corporation and they must all work well together in order to be successful. I assembled a local team to help me with the production of the paperwork, logos, office building, phone system, merchant accounts, etc. This was more work and took more planning than I had anticipated. I decided to use some of Dave's employees to get started because they were already in the building.

Dave and I focused most of our attention on the format of the seminars. Having worked in the industry for years, Dave knew exactly what to expect and how to prevent problems from occurring. One thing to which he was unaccustomed was having the owner of the company out on the road with him, traveling from city to city and teaching in person. He also was not used to the training occurring the same day that the students enrolled, but I wanted to be different. I wanted to put people in business and train them all in one day. This was a first for the seminar industry. Typically, the front-end team arrives in the designated city beforehand and enrolls people in a three-day class presented weeks later. No one did the selling and the teaching in the same day, but that's what I wanted to do. I knew it was a different approach and ran counter to everything that seemed logical in the industry, but I really didn't care. I was paving my own road to success, not following someone else's.

Once we knew the format, we had to create the sales presentation. We spent hours in Dave's boardroom designing the PowerPoint presentation, making sure it was exactly right. It's important to convey to people exactly what you're selling, and we only had about an hour and a half to do this so it needed to be perfect. We spent weeks working together on the presentation before finally finishing it.

Hidden Millionaires Revealed

We had a presentation, a product, a training course that I had developed, and an office building with employees working on miscellaneous things needed for the seminars. Now came the tough part. We needed a way to advertise our seminars and fill the room with people.

For this next stage, we contacted a man named Jimmy DeFalco out of Orlando, Florida, the owner of DeFalco Advertising. He and Dave had met years ago while Dave was working on another project, so he called Jimmy and set up a meeting.

This was my second real business meeting and it was a very important one. Our goal was to convince DeFalco Advertising to pay for the production of a TV show that would advertise our seminars and, in return, we would agree to let them buy all of our media. An agreement like this would save me almost $100,000. There are not many meetings in life where a hundred grand is at stake, so it was crucial that we sell our idea effectively.

When we arrived at DeFalco Advertising, I was introduced to John Dunn, Jimmy's right-hand man. I had to pitch my idea not only to Jimmy, but also to John, and they both had to agree to any deal before we could move forward.

Here I was, 24-years-old with no experience in the seminar industry, pitching my idea to a man who made the Juice Man and Charles Gibbens the million-aires they are today. These two had seen idea after idea and pitch after pitch. It wouldn't be an easy sell, but I was confident in my ability to present this idea. I went into John's office not to pitch him the idea of making a show for me, but rather to sell him on my product.

This approach worked and by the end of

Business Outside the Internet Box

our meeting, I had John Dunn and Jimmy DeFalco so excited about the project that *they* wanted to use my system. I knew before I began that if they believed in the idea, asking them to fund the production of a show would be easy. I had a feeling if they wanted to use my system after a one-hour meeting, so would the people attending my seminars. My theory worked. By the end of our meeting, we had an agreement. DeFalco would produce the TV show in exchange for the media contract.

This was my second successful meeting. I was two for two, batting a thousand outside of my Internet box, and I was beginning to enjoy being the big corporate mogul.

The next item on our agenda was to name the TV show and write the script. I knew what I wanted to do, but I wasn't sure Jimmy DeFalco would agree with my ideas. His opinion was very important as to how the show was to be structured because if it didn't work, there would be no need for media and that mistake could prove costly. I knew in my heart that I didn't want to be the late-night TV infomercial guy jumping around, shouting and promising viewers millions of dollars. I just wanted to tell my story; I wanted to be genuine and approachable when I talked to people. I also didn't want to reveal what my system entailed in the infomercial itself. I wanted them to be inspired to attend the seminar and learn about it there.

My ideas really bothered Jimmy at first. "There's

no way people will come to an event without knowing what it is they're buying before they even get there," he said.

I disagreed. I could tell them on TV that it was an Internet business, but I didn't want to tell them the specifics. I wanted to share that information on a more personal level. I also didn't want to include the tacky testimonials that every other infomercial used. Jimmy didn't agree with me on that at first, either, but I wanted to be different; I wanted to set my show—and myself—apart from every other one on television.

Eventually, Jimmy acquiesced. I guess I was convincing. I *know* I was being sincere. The last thing I wanted was to be another sleazy late-night pitchman. Those people might get some foot traffic, but most viewers will not even sit through the infomercial, never mind sign up for the seminar. I had a real idea and a genuine approach, and I believed in them both.

Once we agreed on those important details, we came up with the show title, *Hidden Millionaires*. John Dunn suggested the name and I liked it. Next, it was time to write the script. DeFalco Advertising hired someone from Florida to write a script based on the information I had provided. At this point, I had no idea how important that script would be, but how could I? I had never been on TV before.

My transition into the seminar business from my Internet box comfort zone illustrates another **Principle of Entrepreneurship: Never Allow Yourself to**

Business Outside the Internet Box

Become Complacent. I was making good money, I had succeeded beyond anyone's realistic expectations, but I was restless to apply the ideas I had learned to other areas. It was important that I continued to strive for success by building my existing businesses and exploring new areas. I resolved to continue with my entrepreneurial career even though I was already successful. A plateau wasn't a place to stop—it was a place to rest before pushing onward.

When the idea came to me, I didn't even know how to begin to plan a seminar but I knew the idea made sense. I wanted to share my ideas; I knew they worked and, based on my experience with Justin and my dad, I was **confident** that I could teach them to others.

Each day when I wake up, my goal is to continue to stay motivated, be excited about creating new things and expand my business beyond the current state. Some days it's hard to maintain the excitement while working and creating new avenues for income. When you make over $150,000 a month, it's easy to become lazy but the best advice I can give anyone who is starting out in business is to *never* be content with the status quo. If you're making ten thousand dollars a month and you only need five thousand to live the way you want, strive to make fifteen or twenty thousand dollars a month. By continuing to grow and never being content, you will build financial security, not merely a sufficient source of income.

Business Outside the Internet Box

Suppose you and your family can live well on five thousand dollars a month. If your only goal is to make just that, you are not building security for your future or hedging against unexpected calamities. Many middle-class Americans are just one catastrophic illness away from poverty. Many others live paycheck-to-paycheck, a layoff away from home foreclosure or bankruptcy. If you strive to earn twenty thousand dollars each month, you will actually earn enough money in three months to live an entire year. That's building a secure future for yourself and your family. In one year, you will acquire enough income to live four years in your current lifestyle. Now *that's* building a secure financial future.

Remember, my father worked hard all his life, was extremely successful, provided well for his family and retired with money in the bank. In one painful moment, it vanished. You can never be one hundred percent safe in this world, but you can be safer and more secure if you work hard and plan ahead. Don't work yourself to death and don't live in fear of disasters that probably won't ever occur, but prepare yourself with as much financial security as you're able.

Also, in pursuing your goals as an entrepreneur, guard yourself against being cavalier about your finances. Too often people jump into business and spend money as quickly as they earn it. While maintaining a lifestyle at a high-income level, they've forgotten the experience of living with less and how to

Business Outside the Internet Box

budget their finances. Markets and businesses change, economic forces beyond our control emerge, and sometimes well-planned and well-managed businesses fail. As a result, the reckless entrepreneur can be back to living week to week just because of lack of foresight or caution. Today, very few nine-to-five jobs in our culture offer the earning potential that an Internet-based business can deliver.

By simply budgeting, living within your means and always saving money, you can build security for yourself and your family should thing change for the worse. *Never allow yourself to become complacent.* The Internet provides equal access to everyone. You don't need a degree to make money online, and there are many financial opportunities if you're aggressive enough to find them, but you must continually push forward, work hard and live with an eye toward financial security.

Chapter Nine
Trusting My Instincts

In March 2007, after months of preparatory work, it was time to film the *Hidden Millionaires* program. Just stepping onto the soundstage was overwhelming at first because, like most people, I had never been on a production set before. I had recently graduated from working inside the Internet box, where I primarily conducted business online and over the phone, to dealing with people in person and operating a real office with employees. I had officially taken the next step towards presenting my ideas before crowds of people. I now found myself sitting on a soundstage with cameras in my face, operators behind them, people scurrying about and a live audience peering at me.

Lights, Camera, Action!

Jimmy brought in some 75 people or so for the taping. I tried to pretend the entire experience was normal, although clearly it didn't feel normal. The idea behind appearing on a soundstage is to act as though you're having just another conversation with someone without noticing that people happen to be moving all around you with cameras and microphones and who-

Trusting My Instincts

knows-what else behind the scenes. Not only was I about to attempt something entirely alien to me, I was about to do it in front of a large group of people. I was also expected to read a teleprompter that contained the words to a script that I'd never seen before, and I was having makeup applied to my face for the first time in my life as well. I was not particularly impressed with the notion of wearing makeup, but they say it's a necessary part of television. Show business is exactly where I was at that point. My ideas were about to be immortalized in the medium of theatre!

We shot scenes, then re-shot them, then shot another scene, and I began to understand why actors would confess that most of the business of acting is boring. There is so much repetition in filming and maybe that was part of the problem. I was "acting" the part of Anthony Morrison, entrepreneur, instead of just being myself and telling my story. I was extremely uncomfortable with this. The script that I was reading didn't feel like me. The words were not words I would use, and I was actually concentrating on reading, as opposed to speaking naturally. I didn't want to read, I didn't want a script written by someone who didn't really know me, I didn't want to play this part and take my cues from a teleprompter. I wanted to just be real and answer the questions honestly.

If the director would have said, "Just be you, Anthony," I would have been fine with that, but I was playing a part and I wasn't comfortable pretending to

Trusting My Instincts

be this person who was supposed to be me!

At the end of the day, I expressed my unhappiness to John Dunn, who was producing the show. "Some of the things we shot may not be used in the final version of the show," he reassured me, explaining how most shows go through a production process that involves editing, cutting, reformatting, re-shoots, etc., and so we moved on.

The next day we visited Justin to film the construction of his home and several other scenes. His was the only testimonial I would allow since he was someone close to my heart. As much as I changed Justin's life for the better, he changed mine as well by being a very moral Christian person and influencing me to lead a good life.

After wrapping up the shoot at Justin's house, we went to my home to shoot a few scenes of my family. It was important for me to have my family on the show, too. All I wanted to do was tell my story, and they all had important roles in it, so my brother, sister, mom and dad were filmed for the show as well.

The day after the filming "wrapped," I could not find a way to relieve my stress. It had been such an ordeal producing the show and I'd been a nervous wreck the entire time. Talking in front of the cameras was a strange experience and the anxiety was overwhelming. I needed to unwind, so I decided to take a quick vacation. I called a friend and we agreed to head to Las Vegas the next day. I just wanted to get away from everything, but I also wanted to reflect on what I had just accomplished. Shooting *Hidden Millionaires* was a huge step in my career and in my life, but the entire experience had been awkward and uncomfortable. Stepping outside of the Internet box was a giant move and I had expected challenges, but *Hidden Millionaires* had been alienating and unpleasant. I wondered, *Is this the direction my career is now headed?*

We landed in Vegas on a Friday and planned to return home the following Tuesday but that Saturday morning, John Dunn called with bad news. He told me that the show was terrible and that I looked particularly horrible in that I looked uncomfortable and stiff on camera. Apparently, at one point during the filming, I forgot to blink for almost two straight minutes and it was obvious that I was reading from a script. John suggested that I immediately fly back to Mississippi to re-shoot the entire show, at least the parts where I was on camera.

No big deal, I thought. After all, it was my show and I was the only bad thing in it. Oh, and did I happen to mention that I was on camera almost the entire time? Other than that, how did you like the play, Mrs. Lincoln?

Take Two

I agreed to re-shoot *Hidden Millionaires* under the

Trusting My Instincts

condition that I could do it without a teleprompter. I wanted it to be just me answering questions from the heart. John agreed, so I caught a flight out of Las Vegas on Sunday.

Now I was on a mission and knew what I wanted to do. I'd been on a soundstage and had seen cameras before, so this re-shoot was technically my *second* time on TV. I had learned the hard way what I didn't want from the experience, and I was determined to do it my way this time.

When I returned to Mississippi, I informally rewrote the script, changing my dialogue to what I actually wanted to say. I took ownership, making the show more personal and more of my own creation. This was the format I had wanted in the first place, but I didn't have enough experience or confidence in show biz to insist upon it from the get-go. Now I knew how I wanted the show to look and sound so I threw the script away and started over on my own version with the assistance of John Dunn.

The finished product was a wonderful show with a great storyline and a lot of useful information. The re-shoot corrected all the problems of the original, and I felt and looked more comfortable and confident. This time I wasn't *playing* myself—I *was* myself. The new *Hidden Millionaires* show featured my interviews as well as interviews with my dad and Justin. It contained real information from real people describing how my system had changed their lives and the lives of people around them. *That* was what I wanted to achieve with my show. Dave and I just casually talked on camera, and I told my story the way I would if I were talking to a stranger at the mall.

DeFalco was not happy, of course. They had a fifty percent investment in this venture and stood to lose money if it tanked. They were the experts in the business, after all, not me—but I knew people would respond to my honesty, the candid way I was telling my story and the fact that I wasn't trying to pitch them. The actual seminar subject wasn't even mentioned in the interview, just my story. This is an unconventional approach to producing what is essentially an infomercial, but it actually worked and we ended up producing a brilliant piece of television that evoked an overwhelming response once it aired. Now, I am not an actor so it wasn't the performance that generated the rave reviews. I received positive feedback simply because I came across as genuine. This is because—surprise!—I actually *am* genuine. This time I was excited by the results of the shoot rather than appalled, and now it was time to test the idea.

My First Seminar

I now had all the necessary tools and pieces in place to proceed. The show was in the can, the office was up and functioning and my staff was busy coordinating our efforts. The paperwork, the media buyers,

Trusting My Instincts

the presentation, the training materials...I now had everything I needed. Everything, that is, except a merchant account, which I found is difficult to obtain, particularly in the seminar industry. Unfortunately, it looked as though my first seminar would have to proceed as planned minus our means to accept credit cards. This was an unexpected problem but I wasn't going to let it stop me. I'd come this far and was determined to make it to the finish line.

I scheduled our first seminars for April 17-19, 2007, and we went to three different cities in South Carolina. This was my first attempt in a new industry, one in which many people failed. The seminar industry is challenging. It's difficult to get people to show up, and it's even harder to convince them that what you're selling has real value. There are so many people out there doing it and large majorities of them are charlatans and frauds but I was determined to make an impact.

The first day was a real eye-opener. We arrived in South Carolina optimistic, but the odds were against us, particularly since there was no way for us to process credit cards. When I saw all the people piling into the room just to listen to what I had to say, I was jubilant. There were so many of them! My idea had become a reality!

The success of those three days in South Carolina taught me many valuable lessons. Ironically, the success of those seminars almost prompted me to stop them just as I was getting started because people told me such terrible stories about their lives that I felt overwhelmed. Many of them had taken busses just to attend, and there was one man who had walked for miles just for the opportunity to meet me. These individuals were real people who truly needed help, and they all seemed to have stories to which I could relate. There were stories of heartache, pain and hopelessness, similar to what my dad had gone through, and there were so many of them.

I left South Carolina with a heavy heart. I didn't know if I was tough enough to handle the world's problems. To be a good and effective teacher, one must also be a good listener, and listening to these stories literally broke my heart. As life affirming as helping people was, it simultaneously left me feeling damaged. The experience had taken so much from me, I returned to Mississippi a changed man, unsure if I wanted to continue conducting seminars.

The Teacher Is Inspired

I took the next month off to reflect on where I was and what I was doing. During that time, I did a lot of soul searching and praying. I wanted to be sure I was doing the right thing for people. I also wanted to be certain that what I was doing was right for me.

At the end of the month I decided to give seminars another shot, so we booked Orlando, Florida, for my second event. What a difference it made! By this time, we had a merchant account so we could finally accept credit cards, and the stories told to me by the people who attended were very uplifting as opposed to depressing. I didn't hear tales of horror and sadness, but of happiness and excitement. They saw there was possibility for improvement in their lives; my ideas fed that optimism, and that optimism fed me. I began to realize that my story had more than one audience. It touched those who were down on their luck, but it also inspired those who were financially secure yet still looking to improve their lives. I was affecting all kinds of people in different ways by simply teaching them what I knew and it was gratifying.

The one negative experience was that I discovered some unpleasant aspects of scheduling seminars—the hard way. In the Orlando market, we scheduled events in three different cities on three different days. One particular day in Daytona Beach, no one showed up at our evening seminar. I was baffled. How could this have happened? Typically, at least a few people always made an appearance. Eventually I learned that even though the weather was cooperating, the bridge from the mainland was closed that evening due to high winds. This was my first lesson in preparedness. Being aware of your surroundings is important, especially when planning an appearance. Everything from weather to traffic patterns and parking availability can affect the outcome of your event.

Trusting My Instincts

The Florida seminars left me with a much more positive outlook on my venture because I realized I could make people happy and give them hope and, if nothing else, I could motivate them to persevere. The funniest aspect of this experience was that everyone, and I do mean everyone, was shocked to see *me*. On the show, I stated at least ten separate times that I would be conducting the seminars in person, but people simply refused to believe it until they actually saw me in the flesh. It's simply not done in the industry. Most folks are excited to meet someone they saw on TV in the first place, but seeing someone you honestly never expected to meet makes them even happier. It's welcoming to attend an event where so many people are excited to meet you and listen to what you have to say.

This became my life. I traveled by bus from city to city, seminar to seminar, teaching people my ideas and methods, enjoying the interaction and adapting to the vagaries of the business.

Learning While Working

I learned as I continued to work that the seminar industry changes on a daily basis. What worked today won't necessarily work tomorrow and I soon became aware of the fact that we needed to adapt in order to remain successful. In business, complacency can be dangerous, but in seminars, it can be fatal. I had to learn how to buy media, select the right locations for

Trusting My Instincts

hotels, and various other adaptive strategies, all of which affected the business drastically.

The first priority was buying media. When we went to South Carolina and Orlando, before each seminar, we ran the standard overnight commercials on local stations, but our next stop was Nashville, Tennessee, and I decided to change our approach. I wanted to run our infomercial during daytime slots and primetime slots. I wanted to be on ABC, NBC, CBS, Fox and CW, and I wanted to be on in the middle of the day and early in the evening. I knew this approach would allow me to reach my target audience and dramatically increase attendance. The media company didn't like my idea because they were skeptical and didn't want to vary from what had always been a successful formula. Nevertheless, I wanted to be different, not for the sake of being contrary or because their formula didn't work, but because I knew in my gut that my approach was *better*. I insisted that we try my approach, and they finally agreed.

Our three-day event in Nashville was our first huge success. We saw hundreds and hundreds of people, more than we had seen in South Carolina and Orlando combined. It was amazing! My idea to change our approach to media buying had been successful. Was it a different approach than the industry standard? Yes. Was it a more expensive approach? Absolutely. It worked, and that was all that mattered to me. For the rest of that year we booked *Hidden Millionaires* in city

Trusting My Instincts

after city, covering the southeastern part of the United States. We could have traveled further, but I wanted to stay close to home so I could see my parents every weekend. Even with regular stops at home, the tour became grueling, and in the midst of all the traveling, I began to realize that I now had a job. It was not a nine-to-five job that left my nights ands weekends free, but a job that was intensive, time-consuming and exhausting. I would miss birthdays and special events at home for the first time in my life because I was obligated to be somewhere else. Also, for the first time in my life, I didn't have one hundred percent control over what I was doing and that disturbed me, but I pressed on and continued my tour.

I was beginning to love teaching and meeting people across the country and I enjoyed the "classroom" experience so much that I began teaching my students about domain investing just for fun at the end of the seminar. It was another way I had discovered to make money online, and I wanted to share that information with the people at my seminars. The response was phenomenal. People were just as excited about domain investing as they were about my system, so I went back into the studio and filmed a full-course DVD on domain investing. I began distributing that DVD as a gift to everyone who came to my seminars.

After being in the seminar business for just one year, I was the proud owner of one of the most successful seminar companies in the business. I had conquered an industry that only people with extremely thick skin dare to enter, and made many connections around the country because of my venture. As we'll discuss later, networking is critically important in business since there are many benefits to building relationships. For example, there are so many ways to utilize quality people that you've worked with before repeatedly. As my seminar business expanded, I would eventually do just that.

Go With Your Gut

My seminar venture is an example of another **Principle of Entrepreneurship: Trust Your Instincts**. I've always been instinctive with my decision process, and those instincts have served me well. This is not to say that decisions that involve great risk, huge investments or potentially life-altering situations shouldn't be given careful consideration. You must have all the facts. You can't swim against the tide when you're unsure of how strong the current is, never mind the fact that there are sharks swimming all around you as well.

In general, I trust my instincts when it comes to making decisions because I have confidence in my ability to make good decisions regardless of prevailing wisdom or whatever the particular industry standard happens to be.

I trusted my instincts with Cool Blue Performance, knowing I could not only compete in the auto parts industry but also dominate it. I knew operating 24/7 was my advantage over my competition. I trusted my instincts with my TV show in regards to not having testimonials, not using a script, and not revealing the actual product. I not only refused to give in to convention when it came to formatting the show, I restructured and made it completely different from any other infomercial on the air. My instincts told me to make the show a personal story that refrained from mentioning the seminar content as opposed to the usual gimmicky sales pitch of other infomercials. My approach worked not in spite of what I had done instinctively, but *because* of it.

I also created a seminar so completely different from any other: I came in person, rather than delegating events to others, I actually put people in business instead of merely selling them business ideas, and I accomplished this by the time they left the seminar. These concepts were innovative approaches never before attempted by anyone in the seminar business but I knew by simply being there that I would demonstrate my confidence in the system and its ability to generate revenue. These things went against the grain, but I **instinctively** knew they would all work, and they did.

I also trusted my instincts when it came to buying media. *Hidden Millionaires* is probably one of the only infomercials—if not *the* only one—you will see on the major networks in the middle of the afternoon

Trusting My Instincts

and during primetime. Traditionally, infomercials aren't run at those times since it's not the proven formula for success. I, however, didn't really care what was normal, accepted or proven. I paved my own path for success in the seminar industry, and my instincts told me to run primetime media, so I did. It cost more, but it increased our exposure to the public, in turn tripling attendance at our events.

It was a bold move telling advertising and television mavericks that my ideas were better than theirs but I was right. We all had money at stake but I knew the conventional approach was not the way to go. I learned from experience that believing in your capabilities over conventional choices and trusting your instincts is the best avenue to success. I know I'm the best advertisement for myself, and no scripted work of fiction could ever convey the details of my story as well as my words in my own voice could.

The corollary to the principle of **Trusting Your Instincts** is that with a proven record of success, an understanding of business and justifiable **confidence**, others will trust your instincts as well. Your record of accomplishment by using your instincts will give others confidence in your abilities. Those who continuously opt to take the safe road may never understand. The essence of every entrepreneur includes a willingness to take risks, but risks based on instinct aren't nearly as incautious as they appear. When your self-assurance leads you to success, others will follow.

Chapter Ten
Investing in Yourself

B y late 2007, I had officially been on the road with the *Hidden Millionaires* tour for a year. Throughout my travels, I had made a number of new potential business contacts, one being a man named Aaron Hoeſt, who attended my seminar in Kansas City, Missouri. At the end of the evening, he handed me his card. That chance meeting would bring me further financial success by providing a springboard into a completely new industry.

Direct Response Partnerships

At Aaron's request, we agreed to discuss a potential partnership between his company and mine. I am the type of businessperson who really wants to see a commitment from someone before I'm willing to agree to work with him on any level, so I decided to test Aaron's commitment level in what he was proposing to me. As it was the week before Thanksgiving, I asked him unexpectedly to fly to Mississippi and meet with me that Friday. I figured that if he was willing to leave home right before a major holiday and on short notice, he was my kind of guy.

Investing in Yourself

To my surprise, that is exactly what he did. Aaron flew into Mississippi and we spent the day discussing possible ways our companies could work together. During the conversation, I mentioned domain name investing. I explained that during my live seminars, I had started incorporating a fifteen-minute bonus session on domain name investing to my students.

Aaron was impressed with what I told him and immediately came up with an idea. Why not produce a direct response TV program and sell a training package on domain name investing? That meeting and conversation set off a chain of events over the following eight months that culminated in the creation of yet another business.

As soon as Aaron left town, I was brainstorming. I knew the idea made sense and the information was extremely valuable, but I had never been in the direct response business. Seminars were a personal endeavor; direct response was something new to me, but I felt ready to give it a shot. I hadn't known much about seminars either when I jumped feet-first into that business, so why not explore the direct response industry?

I immediately contacted LaTesha Burroughs for her expertise on website design and began to think of a name. I wanted the name to be catchy and informative. After days of mulling over the idea, I decided on Invest Domains, LLC. It made sense because I was teaching domain investing. I then needed to obtain the actual domain name, www.investdomains.com. Someone else had the foresight to buy that domain name before me and I ended up having to pay thousands of dollars for it!

Now that I had my business name and domain name secured, it was time to figure out how to start this new business without investing a lot of money. I enjoy spending time on my own ideas, especially if I can get someone else to help me fund them.

I knew what I needed to launch Invest Domains was a great TV show and a great customer service department, so I contacted Jimmy DeFalco, my media buyer for *Hidden Millionaires*. By this time, it had been exactly one year since my first meeting with Jimmy and John Dunn about the seminar company. Their decision to fund my show had been lucrative for them, so I knew I had their confidence. I had also developed a close personal friendship with both Jimmy and John, two great people who are highly respected in their industry. What I love about them is that they truly care about their clients and genuinely want them to be successful. In the business world, it's hard to find people of character so when you happen to come across a few, you stay loyal to them. Again, business connections matter.

I wanted to give Jimmy and John the first option to produce the new TV show for me, so I scheduled a meeting and flew to Orlando to pitch my latest idea to them. My approach was this: I wanted DeFalco Advertising to produce and fund a new TV show to sell

Investing in Yourself

Invest Domains. I also wanted them to be my media buyers and *fund* the media buying.

That was a huge request. If they agreed, I wouldn't be required to put up any money for the show. Their reward would be a percentage of my profits. With this proposal, I was asking them to put even more confidence in me then they had previously but I wasn't worried. Confidence in yourself breeds confidence in those to whom you have proven yourself.

Our meeting took less than ten minutes. Jimmy signed off on the deal, agreeing to invest hundreds of thousands of dollars in my idea in less than ten minutes. Why? There are several reasons, but the main reason was that he was certain of my ability to be successful. I had done just that with *Hidden Millionaires*, against all odds. The second reason was trust. Jimmy trusted me and I trusted Jimmy. It's hard to find people you trust in business because most people are only out for themselves and the almighty dollar. Jimmy knew success was my motivation, not money. I could tell that he was just like me in that he wasn't motivated by money either and thrived on being successful.

To digress from the narrative a bit, I would like to offer some advice for entrepreneurs, particularly novices. Partnerships are generally bad ideas. You won't be reading about me having many partnerships over the next forty years because I like being in control of my own business, ideas and future. However, partnerships with people you can trust and rely on can be

Investing in Yourself

good things. You must be alert and aware, especially if you're new to it, because there will inevitably come a time when someone will try to take advantage of you. That's just human nature, and the nature of business.

Jimmy was the perfect fit for me as a partner. He's an honest and successful man who surrounds himself with people like John Dunn, who are the best in their industries. Trust is a key part of our relationship, and the idea made sense, so we moved forward.

It was time for me to learn about the direct response industry, shoot another TV show, and begin another time-intensive project. I was still on the road with the *Hidden Millionaires* conference tour at the time, so working on a new project was tough. I worked on the Invest Domains project while on the bus traveling to the next city on our tour. There really was no time to waste; I wanted to get started on this project immediately.

The first thing we did was brainstorm on website design ideas and LaTesha went to work. If you visit www.investdomains.com, you will see why she is the best in the web design industry. I then consulted with Aaron Hoeft, who would become my mentor in this particular industry. He knew the ropes and shared a lot of insight as we moved forward. It was not going to be easy, but I was dedicated to investing my time and money into the idea.

Investing in Yourself

Back to the Studio

In April of 2008, I flew into Orlando to shoot my new show, *ProfitNet*. John Dunn once again thought of the show's name. *ProfitNet* would be my second experience in a studio filming a TV show (third, if you count the atrocious "un-blinking man" shoot). This time Jimmy and John both knew what to do. There was no script involved or rehearsed answers, just my simple honesty and sincerity, and I knew everything would work out fine. We brought in two additional people, Chris Hurt and Lauren Thompson, to co-host the show and we flew Burt Anderson in to tell the wonderful story of how domain investing made him wealthy. I had met Burt at one of my *Hidden Millionaires* events in Arizona, and four months later, he was a guest on my nationwide television show.

Chris and Lauren did a fabulous job and the show went very well. Again, I brought my dad in to tell his story because I wanted viewers to realize that I'm a real person with real problems just like everyone else. I simply chose to deal with my problems in an unusual way, one that led me to become extremely successful.

The day after the show wrapped, I was back in the CBS studio in Orlando filming my six-DVD *Invest Domains* training course. This shoot was one of the most difficult challenges I had ever faced because there was no audience and I was presenting a class to nobody!

Investing in Yourself

It wasn't easy but it was necessary, so I wrapped it up that day, having put all my knowledge about this industry into those six DVDs. Now, with barely a breath in between, I was ready to take on the direct response industry. I was only 25 years old.

You Are Your Best Investment

The success of each of my successive businesses substantiates yet another **Principle of Entrepreneurship: Invest in Yourself.** There are many ways in this world to invest, and I could have taken the profits from Cool Blue Performance and invested in the stock market. My father was an experienced real estate investor who took the money he'd earned and invested in the stock market. While real estate and stocks are traditional American ways of investing, they're not guaranteed to succeed, and they're not necessarily the best ways to make more money. The best way to earn income in today's world is to reinvest in your own businesses and continue to look for new ideas and new ventures in which to invest money.

I have always invested in my own ideas and myself. Each business I start gives me the ability to see the world of business from a different perspective and to devise new ways to continue to grow as an entrepreneur. Given the opportunity to invest my money in the stock market or real estate, I'd gladly pass and opt instead to invest in myself.

Investing in Yourself

It's human nature to strive to reach a level of success where money is plentiful and there's time to relax and enjoy it, but at this juncture, the aggressive entrepreneur invests both his time and money into furthering his business interests. There is no logic in earning money yourself only to invest in someone else's business or in an unpredictable public market. When your money is on the line, it always pays to invest in yourself. If there's no money on the line, then invest your time. The return will be worth it.

Chapter Eleven
Building a Reliable Network

Automaker Henry Ford once sued a journalist for calling him stupid in print. At the libel trial, the journalist's attorney asked Ford a series of questions, and Ford was unable to answer any of them. Convinced he'd proven that Ford was indeed ignorant, the attorney pointed out that for a man who controlled a business empire, Ford didn't seem to know very much about it. In response, Ford simply smiled and replied, "I don't need to know those things. I pay people to know those things for me."

No Man (or Woman) Is an Island

There's no question that knowledge is power. But no one person can know *everything*. Even Albert Einstein had his wife assist him with math equations. People who are experts in their chosen professions can assist even the most knowledgeable and capable entrepreneur in managing his business. A network of supporting players is an essential part of the framework of any successful business empire.

I'm no different in that regard because, as curious as I am, as focused as I am on learning the nuts and bolts of every business, I still rely on others for their skill and insight to make my businesses run. It's no accident that successful people seem to associate with other successful people. They tend to run in packs! The basic characteristics of most entrepreneurs are similar no matter what business they're in, and the more you network with others, the better prepared you will be in every possible situation.

Yes, my first serious foray into business was mostly a solo venture but even under those primitive conditions, I wasn't alone. As you know, before I could even process my first order, I needed to establish a killer website, and through networking, I was able to make a connection with a very special individual who would help me innumerable times over the next few years.

The Incomparable LaTesha Burroughs

I didn't know anything about LaTesha Burroughs when I first contacted her about designing the Cool Blue Performance site. Like me, she was using the anonymity of the Internet to help her conduct business. I had no way of knowing she was actually younger than I was or anything about her background. Without the benefit of the Internet, it's unlikely I ever would've met her, but she proved herself a master at web design, and we eventually became close friends.

When I was going through an emotional breakup

with my girlfriend of six years, LaTesha was the one who got me through it. She stayed on the phone with me and talked for hours. It may seem odd that, at that point, we had never even met, but we talked about my relationship and life in general and established a bond both professionally and personally. We live in an amazing age. Technology allows people to become close without even meeting each other in person. LaTesha remains a business associate, friend, and an integral part of my network for success.

A "Gearhead" and a Good Friend

As I mentioned before, Charles Warren was a fellow gearhead I talked with online while in the throes of my supercharger business. Eventually, I persuaded him to drive from Lubbock, Texas, to work on my Mustang, which he did free of charge. We stayed in touch, and when I needed more work done on my car, he came back on numerous occasions. We talked cars and, like me, he appeared to be another working-class car guy. It wasn't until later that I discovered that Charles didn't simply work in a Sonic, he actually owned Sonic restaurants in Texas, Oklahoma and South Carolina.

Charles remains a good friend. I was invited to his wedding, I've taken trips with him, and the personality traits that brought us together when I was in high school remain the foundation of our friendship. Now that he's thinking about expanding his

Building a Reliable Network

Sonics chain, I'm thinking about investing in the venture. We bonded over cars, but made our ways in very different businesses and here we are today with an opportunity to collaborate in the restaurant business.

The Dream Team

When I decided I wanted to teach seminars I went to Dave, the top seminar man I could find. When Dave wanted to produce a TV program, we approached Jimmy DeFalco at DeFalco Advertising, one of the best media companies in the United States. The *Hidden Millionaires* seminar tours depend on the talents of both Jimmy and John Dunn. Cool Blue Performance depends on my dad's management skills and on merchant processing, which is why I hired expert Joe Misiti to handle that aspect of the operation. I hired my lifelong friend Josh to be the Chief Operating Officer of Affiliate Income, and he's great at what he does as well.

It's been said one should hire employees based on personality traits and learning skills, and I believe it because people with the entrepreneurial mindset can learn virtually anything. In many instances, I've always initially worked with people because they demonstrated certain abilities I sought, but I'm finding that often those skills go hand in hand with a vision that's compatible to mine.

Building a Reliable Network

Even though I started small, I was never entirely alone. No one is a success in a vacuum. We all rely on others to enhance our achievements. I not only recognize the abilities of others, I try to keep them in my personal circle, calling on them whenever I need help, both personally and professionally.

This is another one of my **Principles for Entrepreneurship: Build A Reliable Network**. You're only as good as the people you're working with in business. I've managed over the years to surround myself with the absolute best people in every industry, and I maintain those relationships and continue to seek out those who share my vision and drive to succeed.

A corollary of this principle is to surround yourself with people you trust. These people will always keep you grounded, give you good advice and provide you with a refuge from the stress of the business world. This isn't the same thing as surrounding yourself with yes-men. They're a dime a dozen. Surround yourself with people who have your best interests at heart, not because you're paying them, but because they are vested in the relationship and genuinely care about you.

There's No Substitute for Family

We are all molded from childhood into the people we become as adults. Some people break that mold, but it's only the truly exceptional child who overcomes poverty, abuse and neglect to succeed. I know I wouldn't be as goal-oriented, motivated or confident in myself without certain key people in my life, and I keep them close to me because they helped make me the person that I am today. The people who are closest to me, of course, are my family.

The first person I must mention is my mother. Mothers are priceless to most of us, and mine is no different. She is an amazing woman. When I was a child, she always encouraged me to make my own decisions and take responsibility for my own actions. My mom stopped working when I was born so she could focus on raising me and my brother and sister in a loving environment. Her decision to spend as much time with us as possible strengthened our bond. This is part of the reason I have such an enormous amount of respect for her. When we were children, my mom always spent quality time with us, taking us swimming, vacationing and to other family-oriented activities. Since my dad worked such long hours, she often took over the additional responsibilities of a father. My mom accompanied me to baseball and karate practice and even took me to pick out my first baseball glove.

I think the most important lesson I learned from her is that you can do anything you want in life as long as you put your mind to it. My mom has succeeded with everything she's attempted because she refuses to fail. I definitely wouldn't be who I am today without her by my side every step of the way.

Building a Reliable Network

Secondly, I must mention my father. He was a generous and loving dad to me when I was a kid, providing me with the newest toys, best games and best overall quality of life. My dad has consistently supported me in everything I ever wanted to do. For example, he let me buy stocks when I was just twelve years old. Most people would think he was crazy for letting a twelve-year-old boy purchase stocks or a teenager organize road trips to collect baseball memorabilia, but my dad always believed in me and never dismissed my dreams. He now runs Cool Blue Performance for me because he's a great businessman in addition to being a great father.

Because of my dad, I grew up to become a confident adult. He was the first person to believe in me, and I thank him for instilling in me certain values that serve me well. Self-confidence is the most important thing an entrepreneur must have in order to be successful. It was perceptive of him to realize that instilling confidence in me at an early age was crucial to my development as an adult. Like my mom, my father supported me in everything I did, including school, sports and business. I can't think of a single moment that my father doubted me or my abilities.

Dad always taught me that a person's character defines who they are, and good character was a defining trait he always wanted me to have.

Building a Reliable Network

Surround Yourself With Good People

You can't pick your family, of course, and I am very fortunate to have a good one but from the time you're old enough to make decisions, you're also capable of surrounding yourself with good people. It's not just a principle for business but a mantra for life for all happy and successful people. Those who lead and follow you, those who advise and befriend you, those upon whom you rely for emotional support or business advice or spiritual guidance are essential in life. These people and the quality of their individual and collective character define who you are as a person.

You can luck into a great family and you can inherit money, but you can't expect to be handed entre-preneurial success or a great life. Successful people make it all happen themselves and, as a result, they are able to be *selective* when choosing the individuals who will work with them and who will be closest to them.

Chapter Twelve
With Success Comes Responsibility

Many wealthy people will tell you that giving back is critical. There's certainly precedence in the notion that the rich have a responsibility, a noblesse oblige, as the French called it, toward their fellow citizens. Not everyone believes in this idea, but it's one I endorse wholeheartedly. Giving back is an essential entrepreneurial principle. It's easy to be skeptical of such statements and many would say, "Sure, it's easy for *him* to say we should give back when he's got all the money." It's a valid point, if money is the only asset you believe you possess.

Pay It Forward

People are capable of doing much more than signing checks and dropping them in the mail, and our value as human beings is far greater than the sum of our bank accounts. We have arms, legs, and voices, and there's no shortage of ways to give back if you're willing to make the effort. Generosity isn't a quantifiable trait, but if it were it would be measured not in dollars and cents but in how much thought and time we give.

That said, those who have had a measure of

success should find ways to put their assets to good work in charitable ways. It wasn't long ago that my family was on the brink of financial ruin, so I'm aware that economic calamity might be only one step away. My goal in studying to become a doctor was to help people, and my goal in teaching my seminars is to empower my students so that they might fiscally improve their lives. I was raised to empathize with the underdog, to help people when they are in need and to empower them when I'm able. To me, giving back isn't an obligation prompted by guilt; it's a mindset to which I'm completely committed, so much so that I started a foundation for underprivileged children.

My charitable organization has its origins in a tradition started by my mother when my brother, sister and I were children. As I explained before, when we were kids, every year we would go to the local shopping mall and pick children's names off the Angel Tree, for whom my mom would buy gifts. These children come from circumstances that often leave them with nothing to open on Christmas morning. The idea of children feeling left out at Christmas hurt my mother deeply. It was our way as conscientious middle-class people to help those in need or in crisis through no fault of their own.

Bustin' Out the Santa Suit

It was several days before Christmas 2006, and I

With Success Comes Responsibility

decided I would go to the mall and check out the Angel Tree. I was finally in a position to give back to others generously and it was something I always wanted to do, so I decided to select a few of the angels from the tree. My mom had mentioned that the older kids, particularly the boys, weren't being selected. Her theory was that because most of the people shopping for Angel Tree kids were women, they preferred buying gifts for little girls. My goal was to buy gifts for the kids who probably wouldn't be picked by anyone else.

When I arrived, I saw there were twenty-three angels left on the tree, and it was two days before Christmas. I inquired as to what would happen to the kids who weren't selected. The woman in charge explained that typically they got nothing. If they received anything, it would be leftover donated toys. That really hit home and it broke my heart to think that a child was going to receive "leftovers" for Christmas, if he got anything at all.

In my family, Christmas had always been such a wonderful day and my parents made every effort to make it perfect for us each year. I decided at that moment to take all of the remaining angels. I knew in my heart that I would not be able to sleep knowing these kids had nothing or "leftovers" on Christmas when I could've done something about it.

When I left the mall, I was faced with a huge problem, one I hadn't thought about when I'd made my decision to take all the remaining angels. I had twenty-three children to buy gifts for, and the last time I'd been in a toy store was ten years earlier. How would I be able to get this done? It was one thing to have a generous impulse, but this would be difficult. I started to panic as I read some of the gifts these kids wanted. They were asking for bikes and Play Stations, games and clothes, and I realized there was no way I could buy everything I needed in twenty-four hours.

When I arrived home and my mom saw me with all those tags, she burst into tears. I wanted to follow through on my impulse, but there was no way I could get everything done myself, so I decided to call in the troops, recruiting some of my friends and family to help. It was a Friday night, right before Christmas, and I didn't expect much of a response. After all, how many young adults want to spend a Friday night buying toys for strangers? To my surprise, I was able to gather a group of people together to help. Among them were my good friend Josh Siegal, my good friend Sammy Chandna, who happened to work at BestBuy, my brother Adrian, his girlfriend Kaci Dempsey, and my good friend Anthony Battaglia.

We all made our way to Toys 'R Us, WalMart and the local mall, buying everything we needed in order to give these children what they wanted. Each child had filled out a card listing a few items they really wanted with expectations of receiving one or two. Instead, we got them everything on their lists, plus anything else we could find that we thought they might enjoy.

With Success Comes Responsibility

The experience was about making a child happy, giving generously, not giving the bare minimum, and if we were going to do it at all, we were going to do it right.

At the end of the evening, we had to return home and tag every gift. It took hours to complete. We also realized that we needed batteries, so Sammy used his BestBuy discount and got us a great deal on all the batteries we could carry. We gathered in the spirit of giving that night, knowing that we had helped twenty-three children have a wonderful Christmas morning.

Christmas for Kids

I learned something that night, something that stuck with me and actually inspired me to continue Christmas For Kids every year. I watched as young adults gave up partying and hanging out on a Friday night to give of their time and themselves to help others. I saw how excited they were and how they were extremely conscientious about choosing the right gifts for these children. They had a genuine interest in it and it made them feel good about themselves, a selfless act that created joy on both ends of the equation.

What started as a spur of the moment generous impulse blossomed into the foundation of an organization. Soon after, our Christmas For Kids story was featured in a local newspaper. Consequently, I began to receive requests and messages on Myspace and Facebook from young adults all over the Mississippi area, wanting an opportunity to participate in this event and pick out presents.

I saw that my story and my spur of the moment decision had inspired other young people to want to give back to those less fortunate. I think most young adults, especially those in college, see money as an obstacle to giving back during the holidays. Many in their early twenties are struggling to pay back student loans and bills stacked to the roof, but I had created an avenue for them to give back and invest emotionally without having to invest financially.

Christmas For Kids became a huge success. Some volunteers even planned to participate the following year by saving *their* money and contributing financially as well. It was so gratifying to see my actions inspire others to take action, and to realize that it's not necessary to be wealthy to participate in the Angel Tree program.

Being a young Internet entrepreneur, I used what I knew to create more interest in and awareness of our mission online. I started a ChristmasForKids.us group on Facebook that allows young people in my area to volunteer for the program. I started a website, www.ChristmasForKids.us, that explains our mission, describes the program, and allows people to volunteer each year during the holidays.

My second year with Christmas For Kids, I chose twenty-four Angel Tree kids for the program. I really

With Success Comes Responsibility

didn't pay much attention to their gift lists because I planned to get them whatever they asked for. When I arrived home with the names, I realized that seventeen children wanted bikes! I think most people have no idea how hard it is to get WalMart to assemble seventeen bikes in one evening, but I certainly do. I had limited time that year because I was scheduled to speak in Arkansas the following week, so I had to pull some strings to make things happen quickly. I put a call into Toys 'R Us and they agreed to open the store one hour early for my volunteer shoppers and me. This allowed us time to get everything we needed, in less time than it normally would have taken.

This time, the media wanted to cover our event so I obliged. I was grateful for anything that generated awareness for our cause. It wasn't about having the spotlight on me, but about changing people's lives in a unique way. Not only was I providing for needy children in our area, I was providing a way for young adults to give back and become caring, compassionate, thoughtful adults. The organization provides assistance two-fold; the volunteers in this program will argue that they get as much out of it as the children who receive the gifts. I know I certainly get great satisfaction from helping so many people in so many different ways, both by giving and facilitating others to give. Christmas For Kids is about filling an emotional void in underprivileged children's lives and providing others with a way to reach out, but a truly proactive charity has to be about teaching people how to better their situation in life. Any future charity I create will come in the form of helping people to better themselves through education or opportunity.

Children Are the Future

In retrospect, Christmas For Kids was the perfect charity for me because I have always had a soft spot for children. When I was younger, I spent many weekends babysitting a beautiful little girl named IsaBell. Her mother, Shanel, was wonderful but her father left them both and never really knew his little girl. I would take IsaBell to the park to see the ducks, and even outside at night to gaze at and ponder the mysterious beauty of the moon. I adored her. I realized at a very young age that children like IsaBell can't help the situation they're born into. I babysat for IsaBell from the time she was born until she was four years old, creating a bond between us that was very strong. IsaBell couldn't know this, but she taught me many lessons about children and compassion that inspired my desire to help children.

Giving back isn't just about feeling better about yourself. It's not about how much you give, but rather what you give. It's about making decisions that have a constructive element. Looking back on that first computer my parents gave me, my ability to get on the Internet and learn gave me an advantage over every

With Success Comes Responsibility

kid who didn't have a computer, so I'm brainstorming on ways to provide underprivileged children with computers and set up scholarships for children who can't afford to attend college. When I give a child a computer, I'm investing in his ability to learn what I know and become financially secure. When I pay for a child's education, I'm investing in that child so she has a chance to be financially secure. If I give a kid a skateboard, I'm not helping him defer time he could be using to learn; I'm actually enabling him to experience play and use his imagination. It's all good.

Empathy is an amazing emotion and teaching children how to empathize is every parent's obligation. Why did my mom cry when she saw that I had taken all the remaining Angel Tree tags? I know it's partly because she's a compassionate soul who genuinely feels for people who live with deprivation and pain. Like most people who have overcome adversity, it's given her a greater appreciation for her own life and good fortune. I also think that part of her emotional outpouring came from her realization that as a mother she had succeeded in teaching me compassion. In her role as a parent, in the countless hours she'd spent leading by example and with her own voice, she had found a way to give back to the world by raising empathetic children who care.

I am yet to become a father with children of my own but in the meantime, I've made it my mission to be an example to others, particularly successful young entrepreneurs. None of the monuments that you build to yourself will inspire you the way having an impact on one child's life will. By giving back, we learn to be generous with our hearts and spirits as well as with our bank accounts. Knowing that I have made a few lives just a little bit better gives me more satisfaction than any business venture ever could and reminds me that we all have the capacity to help others in our own way. That capacity, that responsibility, is an integral part of life as a successful person.

As an entrepreneur, you must prepare yourself for success, picture yourself succeeding and never think of any other potential outcome. You should also prepare yourself for the responsibility that comes with your newfound success. Giving back is more than a monetary gesture; it's about committing to making the world a better place. For those who have succeeded financially, giving back can be all about volunteering, but it's also an opportunity to use your money in a conscientious way.

A Life Less Ordinary

When my business ventures started to take off, I quickly realized that having money and success enabled me to lead a life less ordinary. For one thing, success has enabled me to provide and care for my family in ways that perhaps other people can't due to a lack of resources. My first priority was always

With Success Comes Responsibility

my family. Because of my success and my less than ordinary life, I am able to take care of the people who matter most to me.

With success comes a responsibility to help others in every way you possibly can. This begins with those closest to you and extends to those who rely on you and the people who work for you. Money, after all, is only as valuable as what it represents. Success enables you to care for people the way everyone deserves to be cared for. It also puts you in a position to give back by sharing information.

Information is power, and if you share that information, you share that power. I could stop anyone on the street and hand them a giant check and they would be financially secure for a while, but if I teach them how to navigate the Internet and how to start their own business, their potential for success is unlimited because the key to success is knowledge, and I'm happy to share that as well. Helping people has always been my mission.

When I started, my goal wasn't to give money to a charity or a group representing underprivileged people; my goal from the beginning was to help someone in need, my dad. Today, even after I've earned millions of dollars, I still remember that this all began when someone I love very much needed help. I've purchased many things with my money, but most of it has been for others: I paid off my parents' house, bought my brother a new car, my sister a car, paid for family

With Success Comes Responsibility

vacations, bought my dad a new truck, remodeled our house, and gave money to almost everyone I know for one reason or another. When I reflect on the choices I've made with my money, I know that the best feeling comes when I think of how happy I've made the people in my life. I've been able to remove stress and bring happiness back into their lives again. That's ultimately what success is all about: securing your own future and helping others along the way.

I've always tried to reach out personally to specific individuals but there are people who need help throughout the entire world, and as long as the financially fortunate help them, we'll begin to see fewer people in desperate economic situations.

This is another **Principle of Entrepreneurship: With Success Comes Responsibility**. This isn't to say that successful people are obligated to give away their business secrets or money, but there is a moral obligation to help others. This applies to everyone, but certainly those with greater fortune have a greater responsibility to help.

With success comes the obligation to offer genuine, valuable information to others without manipulating their optimism to further your own pursuits. At the very least it requires that you not take from those who need help and come to you looking for guidance. You are a human being first, not a corporation or a celebrity. No matter how much money you make, you must stay grounded. Remember, you

With Success Comes Responsibility

weren't always successful and you certainly weren't always a millionaire.

Whenever I come off the road from teaching seminars, my mom likes to remind me that I have responsibilities around the house because before I was a successful entrepreneur, I was part of a family, and in a family, everyone contributes. Money can change your perspective, which is why it is crucial to remember where you came from.

In giving back, in opening yourself to helping others, you may make yourself somewhat vulnerable and wonder, *Does this woman want to date my money or me? Does this person like me or is he just hoping I'll invest in his new business?* I'd rather err on the side of generosity than on the side of cynicism and distrust, but ultimately you have to trust your instincts.

Just as each of the prior **Principles of Entrepreneurship** will help lead you to success, this principle will allow you to share your success and maintain your humanity by always keeping you connected to the rest of the world.

Conclusion
Going Forward

Success stories are admittedly heavy on positive experiences; as someone once said, there are no failures at a high school reunion, and similarly there are no memoirs or entrepreneurial how-to books that dwell on failure. I have had a great deal of success in a relatively short period, and I intend to continue to be successful because I believe I understand *how* to be successful and I have the will to continue striving for new opportunities and new ventures.

It's important to remember that failure is an essential part of success. Some people consider failure to be the opposite of success, but those who have a breadth of business experience understand that failure is often a precursor to success, and sometimes a necessary catalyst. Failure is how we learn, and studies show that those entrepreneurs who regard themselves as successful identify an average of three failures per person in their professional past.

Were these successful individuals defeated by their failures? No, in fact it's quite the opposite. Clearly, most of these successful people were inspired and spurred onward by defeat seeing their failures as signs to work harder or be smarter, or both.

Going Forward

It is the rare individual who has sailed through life with no setbacks. It is essential that when you as an entrepreneur encounter failure, you learn from it. Don't dwell on defeat, don't seek to assign blame, and don't run from your mistakes. Learn from what your experiences have taught you, the positives and negatives, and move on to your next venture. I have no intention of backing down when confronted by adversity; I intend to face challenges head on, to learn from my mistakes and to move forward whenever possible with fearless enthusiasm. I encourage you to do the same. Remember, we are all self-made, but only those among us that are truly successful ever admit it.

So what comes next for me?

I know I'll continue to grow as an entrepreneur, both within my existing businesses and in other areas that I find interesting and challenging. I do not yet know what I'll be drawn to or what destinations are ahead of me, but I do know that wherever I go, wherever I land, I'll be sure to apply the **Twelve Principles for Entrepreneurial Success**. Use these principles as a guide whenever you need more inspiration, motivation, or a good, old-fashioned kick in the butt!

Develop an Entrepreneurial Mindset

Develop the attributes of **knowledge, motivation, confidence, strategies** and **resourcefulness**. Apply these

Going Forward

attributes to all of your business endeavors.

Know—knowledge is power, and now that you have completed this book, you have acquired new knowledge. You have learned what is required to maintain the entrepreneurial mindset that will lead you to success.

Know—the difference between a successful person and an unsuccessful person is how they each react during difficult times. Successful people always think positively and are motivated to succeed and better themselves, and all successful entrepreneurs have confidence in themselves and a motivation to succeed.

It's true that some people are born with an ability to "think" like an entrepreneur, and these people have a definite advantage, but this way of thinking *can* be learned. It is simply a matter of following established principles and applying them to every endeavor. Anyone can be taught to think like or train themselves to think like an entrepreneur, and whether you're born with it or acquire the skill, once you have the right mindset and master these basic principles, success is just steps away. Whether you are driven by entrepreneurial spirit or by a desire to improve your existing life and work situations, these principles are applicable to life in general.

New Ideas Are All Around You

Know—things you're passionate about can be the best businesses ideas, especially hobbies, because your knowledge of the subject and your enthusiasm for what

Going Forward

you're doing is more inspiring than money. I knew my customer base with Mustang parts because I *was* the customer base, and my **knowledge** and enthusiasm led me to greater success than those who lacked my understanding, passion and dedication.

My hobbies became my businesses because I wanted to enhance the things I already enjoyed doing. Sometimes the simplest and most easily engineered business ideas are just lying there, waiting to be discovered. I, for example, discovered that I could sell the baseball cards I purchased online at trade shows in my area at a profit. It was a complete accident, but from the first time my father took me to a card show, I knew I could succeed in that environment. The fact that the other vendors were older men, mostly retired, didn't intimidate me; in fact, because I pursued the notion of selling cards at an age when most boys are simply collectors gave me an edge, because the fact that I was a kid plying a trade amongst grown men made me an instant draw at the shows. Most of the collectors were kids around my age, so I wasn't just selling to the demographic—I *was* the demographic. I had discovered a new idea, and maybe I wasn't the first kid to realize the advantage someone my age had in the collectibles market, but I was the first to *act* on it. The process can work in reverse as well. Find an idea that intrigues you, learn about it and follow that happy pursuit of knowledge into business.

Know—the adage that one must do in life what one enjoys in order to succeed is probably true. I truly believe that by doing what you love, you'll always have greater success than if you were doing something purely for money. And don't stop exploring and learning, because there are ideas that you will find exciting and intriguing if you have a sense of adventure and continue expanding on your interests.

Be Aggressive

Know—it's essential to be an aggressive person if you're to succeed in business, and you must apply this principle in every endeavor. At fourteen, I was more interested in funding my private fun than I was in making a fortune, but the principle was already in place. By aggressively pursuing opportunities; refusing to accept "no" for an answer; creating strategies that achieve goals, and eliminating the middleman, I had created a profitable business niche for myself. I went from being one of the kids on the railing at the ballpark hoping for a single signature, or buying the signed bats at the concession stand, to being a vendor of such memorabilia. There were other people who would stake out the hotel where the players stayed, and there were others who were aggressive, but I managed to create my own business opportunity by combining friendliness and politeness with an aggressive approach to obtaining merchandise. I didn't think of these people as such, but they were my competition, and by being aggressive I found a way to outperform my competition.

Going Forward

By the time I started Cool Blue Performance, I had mastered the art of pursuing goals to their logical conclusion. That was my first "real" business, but I had practiced my tactics for years without realizing that I had created a model for entrepreneurial behavior. In all of my ventures, I have aggressively pursued opportunities, refused to accept "no" for an answer and created strategies for achieving goals. In virtually every business I have started, I have reacted to obstacles by circumventing them aggressively. Only by being aggressive can one surpass the competition that is an inherent part of free-market capitalism.

Strive to Acquire Knowledge

Know—knowledge is everything in business, and an entrepreneur should always strive to learn more. Be an expert in your field.

I didn't set out to corner the Mustang supercharger market, but that eventuality came as a result of me learning everything I could about superchargers, then buying all the used superchargers I saw posted on the Mustang message boards. I was fifteen years old, and because I was knowledgeable about the field and had found a way to maximize the opportunities presented by the online market, anyone looking for a used supercharger online had to come to me. Superchargers cost as much as $3,000, which was more than I could afford to spend even on my own car, let alone on an investment, but I was rolling twenty or thirty superchargers a year, without investing a single penny, and I never once reached into my wallet. All this happened through the power of the Internet and my own enthusiasm and aggressiveness in pursuing the objects of my desire—and I didn't even have a real job.

Know—if you're intelligent enough to become an expert in one industry, you can always teach yourself how another industry works because the ability to learn and apply that knowledge transcends businesses. With new knowledge, you can start another business, and the model is infinite in its applications as long as you continue to seek out information. They say lawyers should never ask a witness a question they don't already know the answer to; approach every business venture with the goal in mind of knowing as much as you can about the business you're entering into.

Don't Be Afraid to Take Risks

Know—you must have **confidence** in yourself or no one else ever will, and your confidence will help sell your ideas and products.

Know—what will separate successful entrepreneurs from unsuccessful ones are the risks they're willing to take. Cool Blue Performance was a risk for me at a time when my family was in crisis financially, but I was **motivated** to succeed by my family's plight and by confidence in my idea's feasibility. I knew the business

Going Forward

wouldn't be easy because I had no start-up money and no credit, so I borrowed one of my dad's credit cards for my setup costs. He was one hundred percent against me going into business for myself but he didn't really have any other viable options at that point, and I was not deterred. I identified Cool Blue Performance as a worthwhile risk because I knew the industry, I had faith in the uniqueness of business approach, specifically the 24/7 access I was providing customers, and I knew how important it was that I succeed.

Anything into which you invest time, money and your self-esteem has an element of risk attached. Take calculated risks that are primarily predicated on your willingness to work hard; self-reliance and a belief in your own ability will supersede the nagging doubts you have about the feasibility of a venture.

I was also taking a risk getting into the seminar industry because I was a novice and insisted on things that ran counter to the industry standard, but I had confidence that my instincts were correct, and they were. Calculate the risks, eliminate them if you can, but don't be deterred by uncharted waters. Historically, sailing into uncharted waters is how early explorers discovered new lands, and great success has rarely been the reward for those who lacked confidence in their own judgment and abilities.

Going Forward

Start Small but Think Big

Cool Blue Performance started small because I had no resources. My goal was to pursue it to its logical end and make it as large and successful as possible. After just one year in business, I decided that CBP needed to have its own line of product. Because I saw that most people consider manufacturers to be the source, as things were, I was technically a middleman and I didn't like the public perception that my company was an intermediary or broker. So I contracted with a company to manufacture my own CBP products. By putting my company's name on products, I was establishing myself as a direct competitor. By the end of that first year, I had done nearly half a million dollars in sales, closing more than 1,300 deals and clearing $76,000. I had accounts with all of the major manufacturers. I was a full-time pre-med student who ran his business part-time from a cell phone and computer, and I still managed to save my family home and my own college education.

Every one of my businesses since has been started with the goal of maximizing its potential. I vacillated on whether to pursue CPB full-time because I was still aspiring to be a doctor, but even in that state of conflict between two viable career options I still pursued both with all my energy. I pushed Cool Blue Performance to the next logical level of success *because that's what entrepreneurs do*, even when I wasn't certain CPB was

Going Forward

what I wanted to continue doing.

Know—if you're starting small with no aspirations of becoming larger, or you can see the ceiling of success as soon as you start, you'll remain small by design. Never limit yourself, because the world will make every effort to do that for you.

Know—an entrepreneur has no restrictions. Set your sights high, begin where you have the resources to begin, and strive to be the best and the biggest. Never doubt yourself, and stay motivated.

Know—your endeavor may involve a lot of work with little or no return, but you must overcome frustration and look to the future. Ask yourself: How successful will I be if I keep working at it? You already know how successful you'll be if you don't work at it.

Know—it's easy to fail, and most businesses fail in the first five years, but if your idea is sound, you'll only fail if you lack persistence. And failure isn't the end, only a detour. As Thomas Edison said after his one-thousandth light bulb prototype worked and he was asked how it felt to fail one thousand times, "I didn't fail one thousand times. The light bulb is an invention that took one thousand steps."

Know—nothing in life is easy or everyone would be wealthy. Anything you try can be an avenue to success, but it requires work, time and effort to succeed. Nothing in the success equation will matter more than your determination.

Going Forward

Balance Work and Life

Know—success requires dedication, and I dedicated every spare minute of my life to getting Cool Blue Performance off the ground. Being finished with school was a tremendous relief because while part of me still aspired to be a doctor, dealing with one full-time occupation after juggling two for the past year and a half was a tremendous relief. I had succeeded with my business, but in the process, I had isolated myself from everyone I cared for. I had very few friends because I simply didn't have time for them and my girlfriend had grown tired of all the interruptions and my preoccupation with work. My success was indisputable, but it was easy to see that my fixation on work was ruining the rest of my life. What benefit was there to being a success if I had no time to enjoy it?

It's been said that no one on his deathbed ever wished he'd spent more time at work, so it's important to push yourself hard when it come to your work but it's equally important to know when to take time for your personal life. All work and no play not only makes Jack a dull boy, it can make him lonely and frustrated, and what good are all the world's riches if you have no family and friends to enjoy them with?

Know—creating balance in your life is for the sake of yourself and those closest to you. Entrepreneurs in particular must understand that being the boss means work is always there but you must also understand that stepping away from your responsibilities is an essential part of living a purposeful and fulfilling life.

Never Allow Yourself to Become Complacent

After several years in business, I was making good money and had succeeded beyond anyone's realistic expectations, but I was still restless to apply the ideas I had learned in other areas. I continued to build my existing businesses and explore new areas. Success is not a reason to stop pursuing your entrepreneurial career.

Being successful on the Internet brought me a great deal of exposure, especially in my hometown. Every time I ventured out around Madison, people would ask me how they could learn to do what I did. I knew that it was impossible to find the time to teach them individually. The idea of helping people get started in business, and teaching them how to control their own economic fate, was intriguing. I decided that it would be possible to instruct people in groups but finding those interested in learning and getting them together in one place was a challenge. Then it dawned on me: seminars! I immediately began brainstorming and educating myself on the seminar industry and what it took to be successful within that world. I started piecing my thoughts together and made lists of the things I would need.

I was already successful, but I was restless, and the quest for new opportunities and new ventures still intrigued me. It's not enough to have a brilliant idea –great ideas are abundant throughout the world. An entrepreneur does not revel in his success, he seeks new areas to discover, investigate and ultimately conquer. Entrepreneurs are the explorers of this generation, but the uncharted areas that we explore are not geographical; we are discovering ideas and dreams and charting our own futures. If you have an idea, educate yourself on the subject, decide if it is feasible, and then go after it!

Know—a plateau is not a place to stop; it is a place to rest before pushing onward.

Trust Your Instincts

I trusted my instincts with Cool Blue Performance, knowing I could not only compete in the auto parts industry, I could dominate it. I knew operating 24/7 was my advantage over my competition. I also created a seminar so completely different from any other by personally showing up and teaching it, rather than delegating events to others. I also put people in business for themselves as opposed to merely selling them business ideas, and I accomplished this by the time each person left the seminar. These concepts were innovative approaches never before attempted by anyone in the seminar business but I knew by simply being there that I was demonstrating my own confidence in the system and its ability to generate revenue. These things went against

Going Forward

the grain, but I **instinctively** knew they would all work, and they did.

I also trusted my instincts when it came to buying media. *Hidden Millionaires* is probably one of the only infomercials—if not *the* only one—you will see on the major networks in the middle of the afternoon and during primetime. I paved my own path for success in the seminar industry, and my instincts told me to run primetime media whether that was the industry norm or not, so I did. It cost more, but it increased our exposure to the public, in turn tripling attendance at our events.

I trusted my instincts regarding the lack of testimonials and script, and not revealing the actual product in my TV show. I avoided convention in formatting it and created something completely different from any other seminar infomercial on the air. My instincts told me to make the show a personal story, and my approach worked—not in spite of what I had done instinctively, but *because* of it.

I have often gone against conventional wisdom and industry standards, but I have succeeded anyway because I knew each idea would work and they all did. Understand that not all instincts are necessarily intrinsic but are based on acquired knowledge and experiences, not simply guesswork. It's always better to be smart than lucky, and smart people tend to make decisions that make them seem lucky. I have never gone against industry standards to be obstinate- I counter industry standards because the *standard* seems counterintuitive to me, and my alternative seems more logical.

Know yourself and know your gut feelings and you will never go wrong.

Invest in Yourself

There are many ways in this world to invest; I could have taken the profits from Cool Blue Performance and invested in the stock market. My father was an experienced real estate investor who took the money he had earned and invested in the stock market, and while real estate and stocks are traditional American way of investing, there are no guarantees, and they are not necessarily the best ways to make more money.

I have always invested in my own ideas and myself. Each business I start gives me the ability to see the world of business from a different perspective and to devise new ways to continue to grow as an entrepreneur. Given the opportunity to invest my money in the stock market or real estate, I'd gladly pass and opt instead to invest in myself.

It's human nature to strive to reach a level of success where money is plentiful and there's time to relax and enjoy it, but at this juncture, the aggressive entrepreneur invests both his time and money into furthering his business interests. There is no logic in earning money yourself only to invest in someone else's business or in an unpredictable public market. When your money is on the line, it always pays to invest in yourself. If there's no money on the line, then invest your time. The return will be worth it.

Know—the best way to earn money in today's world is to reinvest in your own businesses and to continue to look for new ideas and ventures in which to invest money.

Know—each business you start gives you the ability to see the world from a different angle, a different perspective, and to devise new ways to continue your growth as an entrepreneur.

Know—the aggressive entrepreneur invests both his time and money into furthering his business interests. There are other investment choices, of course, but your best investment is in a venture you yourself control.

Build a Reliable Network

Know—you are only as good as the people you're working with in business. I've always sought out and surrounded myself with the absolute best people in every industry, and I maintain those relationships and continue to seek out those who share my vision and drive to succeed.

As focused as I am on learning the basics of every business, I still rely on others for their skill and insight to make my businesses run well. It's no accident that successful people seem to associate with other successful people. They tend to run in packs! The basic characteristics of most entrepreneurs are similar no matter what business they are in, and the more you network with others, the better prepared you will be in every possible situation.

Yes, my first serious foray into business was mostly a solo venture but even then, I was not completely alone. Before I could even process my first order, I needed to establish a killer website, and through networking, I was able to make a connection with a very special individual in LaTesha Burroughs who would help me innumerable times over the next few years. She continues to be an important part of my network.

Know- to surround yourself with people with whom you are close, people you trust, people who will always keep you grounded, give you good advice and provide you a refuge from the stress of the business world. Those people have your best interests at heart, not because you're paying them, but because they genuinely care about you.

With Success Comes Responsibility

Know—there is a moral obligation to help others through mentoring, donating money or volunteering your time. You are a human being first, not a corporation or a celebrity.

Giving back isn't just about feeling better about yourself. It's not about how much you give, but rather what you give. It's about making decisions that have a

Going Forward

constructive element. When I give a child a computer, I am investing in his future by facilitating his ability to learn what I know and become financially secure. When I pay for a child's education, I'm investing in that child so that she has opportunities for success. If I give a kid a skateboard, I'm not helping him defer time he could be using to learn; I'm actually enabling him to experience play and use his imagination. All giving is good.

My mother taught us to care for others and empathize with the underprivileged, and I sincerely thank her for the countless hours she spent leading by example and in her own voice. In addition to her charitable acts, my mother also found a way to give back to the world by raising empathetic children who care, and I intend to share that legacy everywhere I go.

Know—no matter how much money you make, you must stay grounded and remember your roots. This principle will allow you to share your success and will help you maintain your humanity by always keeping you in contact with the rest of the world. Giving feels good for everyone involved and if more people understood the reciprocal benefits and basic nature of giving, it would be a more common human interaction.

Now comes the moment of truth. It's easy to feel motivated when you finish reading a book or after you leave a seminar intended to motivate you. In fact, starting a business is always exciting and invigorating. To borrow an analogy from my first love, baseball: *It's easy as a pitcher to win on your best day, but can you still*

Going Forward

be a winner when you're not at your best? Ask yourself if you're willing to support your inspiration with the required amount of perspiration.

It's not a level playing field and some of us start with more than others. Some folks are lucky and some get more breaks than others, but remember that success is mostly about applying practical principles to every situation and working hard. In the end, no cheerleader or pep talk will replace real commitment or the insight and energy that must come from you.

Feeling motivated? Inspired? Do you have a great idea for a business?

You have all the tools you'll ever need to succeed at your fingertips. If you also know you have what it takes to be an entrepreneur, then it's time to get started!

Epilogue

From the time I started writing this book until now, so many wonderful new projects have appeared on my horizon that I don't even know where to begin. I started another business that involves DVD production and our first project is a series on investing in domain names, now available as a six-DVD set. After the success of *Hidden Millionaires*, it took me all of seven minutes to persuade DeFalco Advertising to provide one hundred percent of the financing and media buying. In return for this investment, DeFalco is a fifty percent partner in the venture.

In all, I have started eleven businesses in the five years since embarking upon my journey with Cool Blue Performance and I still own and operate every one of them. I'm not in a hurry to part with any of my businesses either; on the contrary, I'm looking to build and expand them.

I have plowed headfirst into fields that I knew nothing about before researching them and have successfully collaborated with experts in industries that were new to me. I have managed to overcome adversity, save my family from financial ruin and explore philanthropic pursuits. I have established a solid foundation that will

Epilogue

support all future endeavors thanks to hard work, determination and a little intestinal fortitude. I have developed a network of capable, trustworthy, like-minded individuals whom I can rely on at all times to operate my various ventures and support my passion and creative vision.

    I am a lucky man—rich beyond my wildest dreams and I don't mean monetarily. I mean that life and all the amazing people in my life are gifts and I have been blessed with many. I am truly grateful and don't plan to squander a single gift or opportunity.

Anthony Morrison
July 4th, 2008

For Additional Information about Anthony Morrison please visit www.AnthonyMorrison.com

Do you have a business idea, but not sure how to get started? Own a business but need help making it profitable? Visit www.MorrisonBusiness.com to find out how Anthony can help make your business grow through one on one consulting.

Index

A
Affiliate marketing 77
Angel Tree 130

B
Baseball 1
Baseball cards 1
Brock, Dr. Hobson 42
Burroughs, LaTesha 51

C
Christmas for Kids 133
Confidence 9
Cool Blue Performance 53
CreditCardInc.com 70

D
DeFalco Advertising 90
DeFalco, Jimmy 90
Direct response partnerships 113
Domain investing 108
Dunn, John 90

E
Edison, Thomas 3
Einstein, Albert 121
Entrepreneur 2

F
Family 13
Father 15
Ford, Henry 121
Ford Mustang 31
Frost, Robert 79

H
Hidden Millionaires 89
Hoeft, Aaron 113
Hurt, Chris 118

I
Infomercials 82
Internet 3
Invest Domains, LLC. .114

J
Jackson, Mississippi 13

K
Khalaf, Justin 76
Knowledge 9

M
Madison, Mississippi 13
Media buying 107
Morrisoneducation.com
Mother 16
Motivation 9

P

Pre-med 43

Principles for Entrepreneurship 3

ProfitNet 118

R

Resourcefulness 9

S

Seminars 7

Sonic restaurants 123

Strategies 9

Superchargers 34

T

The Big Idea 88

Thompson, Lauren 118

Toys 'R Us 31

Trump, Donald 85

W

Warren, Charles 37

WorldCom 45

THE HIDDEN MILLIONAIRE